Writers praise
THE RANDOM HOUSE
GUIDE TO GOOD WRITING

Published by Ballantine Books:

RANDOM HOUSE WEBSTER'S DICTIONARY

THE RANDOM HOUSE ROGET'S THESAURUS

THE RANDOM HOUSE GUIDE TO GOOD WRITING

THE RANDOM HOUSE SPANISH–ENGLISH
ENGLISH–SPANISH DICTIONARY

THE RANDOM HOUSE LATIN AMERICAN SPANISH
DICTIONARY

THE RANDOM HOUSE POWER VOCABULARY BUILDER

THE RANDOM HOUSE JAPANESE–ENGLISH
ENGLISH–JAPANESE DICTIONARY

THE RANDOM HOUSE GUIDE TO GOOD WRITING

Mitchell Ivers

BALLANTINE BOOKS • NEW YORK

Copyright © 1991 by Mitchell Ivers

All rights reserved under International and Pan-American Copyright Conventions. Published in the United States by Ballantine Books, a division of Random House, Inc., New York, and simultaneously in Canada by Random House of Canada Limited, Toronto.

No part of this publication may be reproduced in any form or by any means, electronic or mechanical, including photo-copying, without permission in writing from the publisher. All inquiries should be addressed to Reference & Information Publishing Department, Random House, 201 East 50th Street, New York, NY 10022.

Owing to limitations of space, all acknowledgments of per-mission to reprint previously published material will be found following the indexes.

http://www.randomhouse.com

Library of Congress Catalog Card Number: 96-96198

ISBN 0-345-37996-9

This edition published by arrangement with Random House, Inc.

Manufactured in the United States of America

First Ballantine Books Edition: November 1993

10 9 8 7 6 5 4

For Harriet and Skitch

Good writing excites me, and makes life worth living.
— *HAROLD PINTER*

The Random House Guide to Good Writing is for those who have to write—and wish they could write better; and for those who wish to write—but can't or won't or don't.

Preface

Since Random House was created by Bennett Cerf and Donald Klopfer in 1927, it has taken pride in publishing some of the century's greatest writers, edited by some of the century's greatest editors: authors like William Faulkner, James Joyce, Eugene O'Neill, and Gertrude Stein; and editors like Albert Erskine, Robert Loomis, Joseph Fox, Jason Epstein, and Toni Morrison. Bennett Cerf maintained that a publishing house was defined by the interests and obsessions of its editors and the writers they admired. The house that Bennett and Donald built—a house built on good books—came to represent quality and diversity, and readers came to associate Random House with the best of writing.

The unspoken editorial policy was always to encourage the individuality of the writer, never to impose a "house style." No one would want James A. Michener's writing to resemble Gore Vidal's, E. L. Doctorow's stories to sound like Dr. Seuss's, Julia Phillips's life to be told like Moss Hart's, or Truman Capote's style to dictate Neil Sheehan's. Nor would anyone with any sense dictate rules and conventions that might rob a writer of the very idiosyncrasies the reader most enjoys.

Yet there are principles of style and usage, and guides to grammar and punctuation, that can help the writer reach the reader with more clarity and greater effectiveness. Every writer needs an editor, and the editors and copy editors at

Random House face the daily challenge of deciding when and to what extent to apply our pencils. Each writer is different; each book is unique.

This book cannot be a guide to *taste* in writing; there can be no single standard. It is, rather, a guide to the principles of voice, tone, structure, grammar, usage, and style upon which writing judgments can be made. You may have learned these principles and forgotten them; you may never have learned them at all.

We hope that *The Random House Guide to Good Writing* will help you turn your appreciation of good writing into an ability to write well and develop a writing style that is felicitous, effective, and, most important, your own.

Contents

INTRODUCTION

How to Read a How-to-Write Book

Read this book with a pen and paper at your side—or with your word processor up and humming. While you're still reading, begin to write.

Most of us write because it is not enough merely to be well read. We long to be "well said," to think of ourselves—and have others think of us—as possessing the ability to write. We admire the economies as well as the poetic fancies of our favorite writers and wish that we too could wield words with such flair. We try and are discouraged. In desperation we pick up a how-to-write book. There are books of instruction and books of inspiration. The instructional books are often dull, while the inspirational books often lack practical advice. Both frequently leave you more discouraged than you were before you picked them up. A good how-to-write book will help you *want* to write.

Two types of how-to-write books have given writers comfort over the years. One eschews rules altogether; the other passes them on for what they may be worth. One example of a book that eschews rules altogether is Brenda Ueland's *If You Want to Write*. Brenda Ueland was a writer, editor, and teacher who died in 1985 at the age of ninety-three. An ardent feminist, she believed that "everyone is talented, original and has something to say," and she recommended that women neglect their housework for writing. *If You Want to Write*, first published in 1938 and currently available in paperback, was intended to inspire women whose creative urge had been "drummed out" by too many "unloving know-it-alls": teachers, critics, parents, and husbands. The only good teacher, Ueland maintained, was an encouraging friend who "loves you, who thinks you are interesting or very important or wonderfully funny." Brenda Ueland's words of encouragement to her students were "Tell me more. Tell me all you can. I want to understand more about everything you feel and know and all the changes inside and out of you. Let more come out."

An example of the other kind of how-to-write book, long out of print, is *Playwright at Work* by playwright and director John van Druten. Written in 1953, when van Druten's kind of well-made play was going out of fashion, the book mostly talked about the techniques he lived and wrote by: laws of construction, plot, and dialogue. "I cannot make you a playwright," van Druten wrote, "I can tell you only what I know and think, myself. There will be no rule that is not covered with the phrase 'to suit my tastes.' Those tastes may very well not be yours, as they have often not been those of other people. But they are all that I can write."

The rules and techniques presented in *The Random House Guide to Good Writing* are offered in the same spirit: as tools with which you can fashion your own writing. If you were to attempt any other craft or hobby—pottery, auto mechanics, photography—you would first acquaint yourself with the available tools and then choose the appropriate ones for the task at hand.

"Writing has laws of perspective," said Truman Capote, "of light and shade, just as painting or music does. If you are born knowing them, fine. If not, learn them. Then rearrange the rules to suit yourself." T. S. Eliot agreed: "It is not wise to violate the rules, until you know how to observe them."

* * *

This book attempts to help you turn your appreciation of good writing into an ability to write well: Chapter One defines good writing, as something first to be appreciated, then to be practiced. Chapter Two demonstrates how to establish voice and tone, Chapter Three the principles of structure and plot, Chapter Four formal and familiar styles. Chapters Five and Six review the rules of grammar and usage many writers struggle with. Chapter Seven is on inspiration and perseverance. There are three appendixes: The first is the Random House Style Manual, the basic rules of punctuation, capitalization, grammar, usage, and style used by Random House's copy editors and proofreaders. The other two appendixes are classic pieces of good writing, both of which are outlined in Chapter Three: Emerson's essay "Character" and Poe's short story "The Masque of the Red Death." Finally, there is a bibliography of books on writing and two indexes, including one containing troublesome words and grammatical terms, which can be used for easy reference.

Examples of good writing are used as illustrations throughout this book; most are drawn from American writing, many but not all from Random House writers. British writers, European writers, and writers of other cultures are cited less frequently, not for chauvinistic reasons but to narrow the focus: There is such a thing as good, clean, contemporary American writing style, and it is the goal of this book to help you achieve it.

ONE

Good Writing

We all know what good writing is: It's the novel we can't put down, the poem we never forget, the speech that changes the way we look at the world. It's the article that tells us when, where, and how, the essay that clarifies what was hazy before.

Good writing is the memo that gets action, the letter that says what a phone call can't. It's the movie that makes us cry, the TV show that makes us laugh, the lyrics to the song we can't stop singing, the advertisement that makes us buy.

Good writing can take form in prose or poetry, fiction or nonfiction. It can be formal or informal, literary or colloquial. The rules and tools for achieving each are different, but one difficult-to-define quality runs through them all: style. "Effectiveness of assertion" was George Bernard Shaw's definition of style. "Proper words in proper places" was Jonathan Swift's.

You cannot sit down to write stylish prose — or to write "stylishly" — but you *can* sit down to write effectively. "Style comes only after long hard practice," wrote William Styron, "and writing." Effective prose requires hard work, and even the best writers get discouraged. "We are all apprentices," said Ernest Hemingway, "in a craft where no one ever becomes a master."

All effective writing, whatever the style, has three characteristics: purpose, form, and appropriateness. What makes writing effective when the purpose is to entertain might be inappropriate when the intention is to persuade. What makes for good writing in a comic novel would probably be ridiculous in a business memo.

This is good writing — in a literary novel: The images are simply expressed and carefully chosen, the metaphors are apt, and the language has a lyricism that evokes emotion:

> There is a loneliness that can be rocked. Arms crossed, knees drawn up; holding, holding on, this motion, unlike a ship's, smooths and contains the rocker. It's an inside kind — wrapped tight like skin. Then there is a loneliness that roams. No rocking can hold it down. It is alive, on its own. A dry and spreading thing that makes the sound of one's own feet going seem to come from a far-off place.
>
> — Toni Morrison, *Beloved*

This is also good writing — in an economic history: The language is concrete, the point of view is clear, and the points are well expressed.

> The 1980s were the triumph of upper America — an ostentatious celebration of wealth, the political ascendancy of the richest third of the population, and a glorification of capitalism, free

markets and finance. But, while money, greed and luxury had become the stuff of popular culture, hardly anyone asked why such great wealth had concentrated at the top, and whether this was a result of public policy.

— Kevin Phillips, *The Politics of Rich and Poor*

This is also good writing — in a personal memoir: The tone is thoughtful and the pace reflective.

In Paris on a chilly evening late in October of 1985 I first became fully aware that the struggle with the disorder in my mind — a struggle which had engaged me for several months — might have a fatal outcome. The moment of revelation came as the car in which I was riding moved down a rain-slick street not far from the Champs-Élysées and slid past a dully glowing sign that read HÔTEL WASHINGTON. I had not seen that hotel in nearly thirty-five years, since the spring of 1952, when for several nights it had become my initial Parisian roosting place.

— William Styron, *Darkness Visible*

Reading good writing is the best way to learn good writing. "Read everything," wrote William Faulkner, "trash, classics, good and bad, and see how they do it."

Write with purpose, write with form, write with appropriateness, and soon you will find yourself writing effectively. In time, you will develop a voice and tone of your own and an ability to suit them to your subject matter and audience, and that will be your style.

WRITING WITH PURPOSE

Purposeful prose gets to the point. Without purpose you wander from topic to topic, underdeveloping the main points and overdeveloping the digressions. With a strong purpose, tangential points will amplify, not diminish, your theme, and you will easily see how and where to cut.

Writing with purpose unites the writer and reader with a common goal: to see if we see eye to eye. Take a newspaper column in which the writer's purpose is "to persuade." Within a paragraph or two, you understand the writer's point of view and begin to agree or disagree. By the sixth or seventh paragraph you have formed your own opinion. By the end, either you have had your beliefs validated or you have been shown a new outlook.

If your purpose is to write about politics, you might be writing an analysis of how Washington works, a history of the constitutional issue of censorship, or an exposé of a recent political scandal. Or you could be writing a historical novel about real kings and ministers in fictional settings. Purpose will help you choose a style appropriate to those choices.

If your purpose is to write about the environment, you might be writing a warning of the dangers of our present ways, a history of environmental abuse, or an eyewitness account of the effects of an oil spill. You might be writing a nightmarish fiction of a world without nature or an equally frightening true story of a family whose home has been contaminated with radon.

If you write with no purpose in mind, you will

quickly run into trouble. "Many people who want to be writers don't really want to be writers," said James A. Michener. "They want to *have been* writers." Without purpose you will find yourself wracked on the rocks of writer's block or showing rambling pages to friends of diminishing patience. A strong purpose will enable you not merely to speak out but to say something in particular, something honest and true, something you wish to express as best you can.

Your purpose should be written on a piece of paper and taped to your mirror or writing table; whenever you go astray, let the reminder steer you back to your course. State your purpose as succinctly as possible, in two or three sentences at most. If you have trouble formulating your purpose, your writing will probably show it. You will wander, and the reader will have trouble figuring out what it is you're getting at — because you yourself won't *know* what it is you're getting at. A well-articulated purpose will guide your way.

Successfully settling on a purpose requires defining, redefining, and continually clarifying your goal — all the while eliminating fuzzy intentions and digressions. It's an ongoing process, and the act of writing can alter your original purpose. You have to know when to remain firm and when to be flexible. Dr. Rudolf Flesch, a staunch advocate of writing with purpose, advised in his best-selling *How to Write Better* that "the main thing to consider is your *purpose* in writing: Why are you sitting down to write?" (To which E. B. White tartly answered, "Because, sir, it is more comfortable than standing up.") Purpose is only one of many tools, but it is one that will help you get started and keep going.

WRITING WITH FORM

An articulated purpose will usually suggest a sense of form, but sometimes the form comes first: You want to write a novel or a short story, a screenplay or a play, or perhaps a letter to the editor, a newspaper article, or a magazine article. You might want to work in a hybrid form like the New Journalism—which uses the techniques of fiction—or the nonfiction novel, which uses the techniques of reporting. Perhaps you wish to write in a certain genre: film criticism, children's books, interviews, or science and technical writing. Perhaps you have to write a business memo or a report.

If you know your purpose—for example, to write about the coming national election—you might wish to write in the form of a novel. Yours may be a serious historical novel with real characters, or it may take place in an invented world in the not-too-distant future. It could be a novel about the murder of a public official, a mystery novel with the obligatory murders and a well-worked-out plot. Or it could be an apocalyptic tale of a lawless world, the form of which has an appropriately structureless feel. Your purpose will suggest a certain form.

Say that your purpose is to write about the environment, and you choose to write nonfiction. You could choose to write a letter to the editor, an op-ed piece, a magazine article, or a book-length treatise. Each has a different length and shape, and each is structured differently. Although all structures are bendable — and some are even breakable — a strong structure will give you what Vladimir Nabokov called a "curiously clear preview" of what it is you intend to write. This preview will enable you to imagine what you are writing before you get it down on paper. A structure will help the writing develop: an introduction first, then an example of what the problem is; after that, a solution, followed by a conclusion.

Some forms depend more upon preexisting structures than do others: screenplays and short stories, for instance, must be tightly structured. Other forms, like the novel, can get by with a looser structure. Each form dictates a structure, and within that structure each piece has its own construction. Even when the construction appears loose to the reader, the author has often worked with strong structure during the writing process. "I always know the ending," said Toni Morrison; "that's where I start." A sense of form and structure, discussed further in Chapter Three, will give your writing discipline.

WRITING WITH APPROPRIATENESS

Writers often find themselves staring at the page or screen with the awful feeling that it sounds "all wrong." *For whom am I writing?* is the question that can help determine the appropriateness of your tone of voice. Obviously, a business letter should not have the same tone as a love letter, but often subtler shades are involved. An article on recycling will use one tone if it is being written for a technical journal and another if it is being written for a community newsletter.

If you were writing a television sitcom, you would use a different level of diction than you would if your story were intended for a literary journal. Not that you can't break out of a conventional form, or that you should write down to an audience; rather, certain voices and vocabularies communicate better to certain audiences, and you need to understand the requirements of the forms you choose to write in.

Inappropriateness of tone is an avoidable error. In nonfiction, there are three most common inappropriate tones: excessive formality, out-of-place humor, and misdirected anger. There are times when formality, humor, and anger are appropriate, but all three are easy to slip into. Writing with purpose is the best way to avoid an inappropriate tone. If your purpose is to persuade, you will quickly realize that anger, condescension, or sarcasm will not accomplish that goal.

Excessive formality often comes from an insecurity with one's own authority. By using an over-formal tone — with many large words, long sentences, or technical terms — the writer attempts, usually unsuccessfully, to mask his or her insufficiencies. If you are writing about a technical subject for a technical audience, it is appropriate to use technical terms, but if you are speaking to a lay audience it is not. If your goal is to impress your readers with your expertise, you should speak in clear and unambiguous language that gets your point across. Throwing jargon at readers who are unfamiliar with it will leave them unimpressed — or, worse, bored.

Formality is best used to convey seriousness of purpose: When all else has failed, a formal tone in a business letter can put someone on notice that you are now ready to pursue legal action. Chapter Four will discuss how to use formality and informality to suit your purpose.

Out-of-place humor or excessive friendliness may also come from insecurity, the writer's need for approval. There is nothing as refreshing as a humorous outlook, but joking around to win the reader over will backfire unless the humor is appropriate. The same can be said for sarcasm or irony: Properly prepared for, they can make your point in a devastating manner, but gratuitous sarcasm can be easily misunderstood.

Anger, no matter how deeply and honestly felt, is rarely persuasive; reason combined with passion almost always is. An angry polemic for or against a political issue may move the already converted to action, but it may also alienate those you wish to persuade. No matter how passionately you make your point, anger or disdain will usually get in the way. Chapter Two will examine the tools that determine the sound of your prose.

WRITING WITH STYLE

"Every style that is not boring is good," said Voltaire. In its classic meaning, style includes voice, diction, sentence structure, and the use of allusion, metaphor, repetition, and figurative language. The writing of a "stylist" is generally noted for its clarity, simplicity, and elegance. American stylists include Ralph Waldo Emerson, Mark Twain, H. L. Mencken, Rachel Carson, James Baldwin, E. B. White, James Thurber, Dorothy Thompson, John Hersey, Joan Didion, John McPhee, Peter Matthiessen, and Tracy Kidder. Another stylist, Katherine Anne Porter, objected to the label. "I've been called a stylist until I really could tear my hair out," she said. "And I simply don't believe in style. The style is you."

The simple expressiveness common to all stylists is found especially in the writing of E. B. White, who spent fifty-one years writing for *The New Yorker* and was co-author of the classic *Elements of Style*. The typical E. B. White piece that follows was written in 1969, shortly after astronauts Neil Armstrong and Buzz Aldrin took the first steps on the moon.

The moon, as it turns out, is a great place for men. One-sixth gravity must be a lot of fun, and when Armstrong and Aldrin went into their bouncy little dance, like two happy children, it was a moment not only of triumph but of gaiety. The moon, on the other hand, is a poor place for flags. Ours looked stiff and awkward, trying to float on the breeze that does not blow. (There must be a lesson here somewhere.) It is traditional, of course, for explorers to plant the flag, but it struck us, as we watched with awe and admiration and pride, that our two fellows were universal men, not national men, and should have been equipped accordingly. Like every great river and every great sea, the moon belongs to none, and belongs to all. It still holds the key to madness, still controls the tides that lap on shores everywhere, still guards the lovers who kiss in every lane under no banner but the sky. What a pity that in our moment of triumph we did not forswear the familiar Iwo Jima scene and plant instead a device acceptable to all: a limp, white handkerchief, perhaps, symbol of the common cold, which, like the moon, unites us all.

—E. B. White, "Moon Landing"

What distinguishes a stylist like White is not only the beauty of his expression but also his economy. "Style," said playwright and poet Bertolt Brecht, "is what gets left out."

Stylishness, on the other hand, is not style; it is whatever is currently considered clever or sophisticated or fashionable. It can be found in the pages of glossy magazines and between the covers of certain first novels. Stylish, fashionable writing usually does not survive any longer than fashionable clothing does.

Style should not be confused with idiosyncrasy. In an attempt at "having a style," many an insecure writer looks to the experiments of James Joyce, Jack Kerouac, and Tom Wolfe. "If they can break the rules," the would-be maverick asks, "why can't I?"

James Joyce did much to liberate our contemporary notions of style, but it is almost impossible to copy him. His free writing was grounded in a rich soil of erudition. His knowledge of the classics and of myth is reflected on nearly every page of his work. His prose sings with a Gaelic lilt that breaks free of the old rules he so obviously knows — rules he breaks with such obvious glee to suit his purpose. Moreover,

Joyce did not use his so-called Joycean prose outside of his fiction, as the two extracts below reveal. The first is in the classic Joycean stream of consciousness:

> After all there's a lot in that vegetarian fine flavour of things from the earth garlic, of course, it stinks Italian organgrinders crisp of onions, mushrooms truffles. Pain to animals too. Pluck and draw fowl. Wretched brutes there at the cattlemarket waiting for the poleaxe to split their skulls open. Moo. Poor trembling calves. Meh. Staggering bob. Bubble and squeak. Butchers' buckets wobble lights. Give us that brisket off the hook. Plup. Rawhead and bloody bones. Flayed glasseyed sheep hung from their haunches, sheepsnouts bloodypapered sniveling nosejam on sawdust. Top and lashers going out. Don't maul them pieces, young one.
>
> Hot fresh blood they prescribe for decline. Blood always needed. Insidious. Lick it up, smoking hot, thick sugary. Famished ghosts.
>
> Ah, I'm hungry.
>
> —James Joyce, *Ulysses*

This next passage is from a letter Joyce wrote to Bennett Cerf, his American publisher, thanking Cerf for Random House's efforts on behalf of the book. In it he recounts the legal difficulties his book has had and uses a more prosaic—more *appropriate*—tone. The letter was published as a preface to the Random House edition of *Ulysses:*

> The continental publication of *Ulysses* proved however to be merely the beginning of complica-

tions in the United Kingdom and the United States. Shipments of copies of *Ulysses* were made to America and to Great Britain with the result that all copies were seized and burnt by the Custom authorities of New York and Folkestone. This created a very peculiar situation. On the one hand I was unable to acquire the copyright in the United States since I could not comply with the requirements of the American copyright law which demands the republication in the United States of any English book published elsewhere within a period of six months after the date of such publication, and on the other hand the demand for *Ulysses* which increased every year in proportion as the book penetrated into larger circles gave the opportunity for any unscrupulous person to have it printed and sold clandestinely.

No sentence fragments. No made-up words. No "moo," no "meh," no "bubble and squeak." No Joycean style. Just a letter that says what has to be said. This too is style.

Style, as we shall see in Chapter Four, is neither an involuntary matter nor something you add to the text to "dress it up." Style should not be thought of as an end unto itself. It is a series of choices—of voice, tone, diction, structure, grammar, and usage—that depend upon purpose and appropriateness. Putting style in almost always clutters writing up; removing clutter gives writing style.

TWO

Voice and Tone

Voice, in writing, tells us who is speaking. Tone projects an attitude. Both are dependent upon diction, the words you choose. The fiction writer creates different characters with voice and tone; the skilled writer of nonfiction can employ them as well. Knowing how to manipulate the tone of voice or the level of diction is essential in writing effective prose.

The distinctions between the voices have been blurred in contemporary writing — experimental fiction mixes voices, and the New Journalism of the sixties, seventies, and eighties has developed a highly subjective third person — but the old divisions are still useful as a starting point.

VOICE

The two voices in which prose is generally written are the first (''I am born'') and the third (''He was born''). The voice of the third person is often referred to as the ''omniscient narrator,'' but knowing everything is not necessarily exclusive to the third person. The second person (''You are born'') is used most frequently in letters and books of instruction, although it is possible to use it in fiction, as Allan Gur-

14

ganus did in portions of his short story "Minor Heroism":

> You find that the headaches are because you suddenly need reading glasses. You resign yourself to buying bourbon by the case because it is cheaper and you now have room to store that much, and you have no doubt that it will somehow get drunk up. —Allan Gurganus, "Minor Heroism"

The First-Person Singular

The first person is the voice we use most naturally when relating our own experiences. It is the voice of autobiography, of newspaper and magazine columns, and of some types of narrative fiction. The thoughts and observations are those of the "I"; no outside voice of authority is invoked. The first person is appropriate when a personal voice is preferred.

Using the first person usually confines the writer to what the "I" can know as well as to the diction and tone of that particular voice—whether it is the writer's own or that of an invented character. Sometimes the first-person "I" can be as omniscient as a third-person "he" or "she," as it is in the excerpt below:

> And here I realize I have come almost to the end of this story of a boy's adventures. Who I am in my majority and whether I am in the criminal trades or not, and where and how I live must remain my secret because I have a certain renown. I will confess

that I have many times since my investiture sought
to toss all the numbers into the air and let them fall
back into letters, so that a new book would emerge,
in a new language of being.

—E. L. Doctorow, *Billy Bathgate*

Confining himself to the voice of Billy Bathgate,
E. L. Doctorow paints Dutch Schultz's world as seen
through the eyes of a boy passing from youth into
adulthood. Other characters speak in dialogue, but it
is dialogue as heard and reported by Billy, who may
have misheard or may be misremembering—the
truth is filtered through his perspective. It is just that
possibility that makes a first-person narrative involving. We come to know Billy's world not by being told
about it objectively but as Billy experiences it, from
Billy's point of view. When the first person is used
effectively in fiction, as it is in *Billy Bathgate,* or *The
Adventures of Huckleberry Finn,* or *David Copper-
field,* the connection between the reader and the character is intensified, and an unforgettable character
can be created.

Some fiction writers gain a little distance on their
main characters by using the first-person voice of a
secondary character, like Ishmael in *Moby-Dick* or
Nick in *The Great Gatsby.* This gives the author the
advantage of being able to describe the main character in words and ideas that the main character would
not use, while still involving the reader in the story in
a personal way.

This next passage illustrates first-person nonfiction:

My mother tells me that up to the age of six I had no psoriasis; it came on strong after an attack of measles in February of 1938, when I was in kindergarten. The disease—"disease" seems strong, for a condition that is not contagious, painful, or debilitating; yet psoriasis has the volatility of a disease, the sense of another presence coöccupying your body and singling you out from the happy herds of healthy, normal mankind—first attached itself to my memory while I was lying on the upstairs side porch of the Shillington house, amid the sickly, oleaginous smell of Siroil, on the fuzzy, sun-warmed towels, with my mother, sunbathing.

                    —John Updike, "At War with My Skin"

The first person is appropriate in nonfiction where the author can presuppose a receptive audience, as when the author of a newspaper or magazine column writes for a weekly or monthly reader, or when an expert writes on a subject in which he or she is an authority. In the excerpt above, Updike's point of view is subjective, and his tone is personal. In the case of a how-to book or an article on a medical subject, the first person is often more objective, conveying the author's voice as the voice of firsthand experience.

☞*Try your hand:*
Relate an event in your life in your own words, using the first person. Describe your observations, your actions, your reactions, the things you said, and the things other people said to you.

Now, still using the first person, relate the same event as if you were someone else, a companion or observer. Note any changes in the tone of the narrative with the new perspective.

The First-Person Plural

A somewhat more objective first-person voice is the first-person plural, used by writers of columns like *The New Yorker*'s "Talk of the Town." This style was mandated by the magazine, whose writers had to use it. Some, like E. B. White, disliked it. He called it a "device as commonplace in journalism as it is harebrained" and said that it gave the "impression that the stuff was written by a set of identical twins or the members of a tumbling act":

> We received at *The New Yorker* this morning an exceptionally friendly letter from the publisher of one of the magazines to which we subscribe. It began: "Dear *Time* Subscriber, I hope very much that you will drop in to see us if you are in New York this summer during the World's Fair. As Publisher of *Time* I have always been sorry I could not meet each of our widely scattered subscribers and talk to you face to face, and I know that all our editors feel the same way."
> This expression of warmth puts us to shame.
> —E. B. White, "Readerhood"

Others, like Lillian Ross, relished the "royal we" and developed it into a fine art that borders on high camp. Ross's winding, chatty, first-person-plural sentences are the verbal equivalent of drinks before dinner:

We had a great lunch last week with a great actress, perhaps the greatest of all, in the opinion of many actors and actresses — Dame Edith Evans, who is here for the first time in over a decade and is rehearsing for her first American play, ''Time Remembered,'' an N.B.C. *Hallmark Hall of Fame* production scheduled for February 7th, the day before Dame Edith's seventy-third birthday.

— Lillian Ross, ''Dame Edith''

Note the length of the sentences and the idiosyncratic attitude. This voice is appropriate when speaking for a group of people who share your views to an audience that similarly shares those views. It can, however, sound smug and elitist, and it should be used with caution. But in a newsletter or an annual family holiday update, the first-person plural is often less impersonal than the third person and less egocentric than the first-person singular.

☞*Try your hand:*

Relate, in the first-person plural, the same event you used in the last exercise. Note the change in your tone of voice.

The Third-Person Objective

The first person is the voice we converse in, but the third person is the primary storytelling voice, the voice of the novel and the short story, of the newspaper article, the essay, and most nonfiction books, of the fairy tale, the fable, and the folktale, of the joke

and the limerick, the Bible, the Koran, and the Bhaga-
vad Gita.

The third person can take on a point of view that is
either objective or subjective. In its objective form,
the third person is the voice of the omniscient narrator, the all-knowing storyteller who metes out what
happened, event by event. This is the voice used in
most nonfiction and in fiction that narrates a story.
The examples below all have omniscient narrators
who speak in the third-person objective:

- Now it came to pass in the days when the Judges
  ruled, that there was a famine in the land: and a
  certain man of Bethlehem, Judah, went to sojourn
  in the country of Moab, he, and his wife, and his
  two sons.

  —Ruth I:1 (King James translation)

- There was a man who had three sons, the young-
  est of whom was called Dummling, who was de-
  spised, mocked, and sneered at on every
  occasion.

  —The Brothers Grimm, ''The Golden Goose''

- Dorothy lived in the midst of the great Kansas
  prairies, with Uncle Henry, who was a farmer,
  and Aunt Em, who was the farmer's wife.

  —L. Frank Baum, *The Wizard of Oz*

- Happy families are all alike; every unhappy family is unhappy in its own way.

  —Leo Tolstoy, *Anna Karenina*
  (translated by Joel Carmichael)

This god- or goddesslike narrator, usually unidentified, knows all and sees all and tells what he or she chooses. The third-person-objective voice seems to be detached from the subject matter and dispassionate toward it, and the narrative seems to convey to the reader no more than the facts of the story. In the hands of a good writer, however, the third person can do much more: It can arouse passion, it can frighten, it can amuse, it can persuade — all without seeming to do so.

In nonfiction, the equivalent of the third-person omniscient narrator is the measured and rational manner of the expository essay, like that of Shelby Foote in this extract from the first volume of *The Civil War: A Narrative:*

It was a Monday in Washington: January 21; Jefferson Davis rose from his seat in the Senate. South Carolina had left the Union a month before, followed by Mississippi, Florida, and Alabama, which seceded at the rate of one a day during the second week of the new year. Georgia went out eight days later; Louisiana and Texas were poised to go; few doubted that they would, along with others.

— Shelby Foote, *The Civil War: A Narrative*

In fiction, the third person can be equally omniscient, seeing and knowing everything but betraying no emotion, as in this passage from the opening of Norman Mailer's first novel:

Nobody could sleep. When morning came, assault craft would be lowered and a first wave of troops would ride through the surf and charge ashore on the beach at Anopopei. All over the ship, all through the convoy, there was a knowledge that in a few hours some of them were going to be dead. . . .

A soldier lies flat on the bunk, closes his eyes, and remains wide-awake. All about him, like the sloughing of surf, he hears the murmurs of men dozing fitfully. ''I won't do it, I won't do it,'' someone cries out of a dream, and the soldier opens his eyes and gazes slowly about the hold, his vision becoming lost in the intricate tangle of hammocks and naked bodies and dangling equipment.

— Norman Mailer, *The Naked and the Dead*

☞*Try your hand:*

Take the event you used in the previous exercises and describe it in the third person, from the vantage point of an omniscient narrator. Try to develop a critical perspective that the three exercises in the first person lacked.

The Third-Person Subjective

Sometimes the first person is too personal a tone, and the third person is too distant. In such a case, the third person can take on a subjective voice. The narrator stands both inside and outside. In the third-person subjective, objective description is mixed with direct expression of the character's thoughts or feelings — but without quotation marks and without the pronoun ''I.'' The technique is often associated with Virginia Woolf and James Joyce, but it had been used by earlier writers in different forms. The extract below demonstrates how Woolf used it to display a character's inner thoughts without the character's expressing them.

> What a lark! What a plunge! For so it had always seemed to her when, with a little squeak of the hinges, which she could hear now, she had burst open the French windows and plunged at Bourton into the open air. How fresh, how calm, stiller than this of course, the air was in the early morning; like the flap of a wave; the kiss of a wave; chill and sharp and yet (for a girl of eighteen as she then was) solemn, feeling as she did, standing there at the open window, that something awful was about to happen . . .
>
> —Virginia Woolf, *Mrs. Dalloway*

Evan S. Connell also used the third-person subjective to suggest the inner life of his characters in his twin novels, *Mrs. Bridge* and *Mr. Bridge*. In the excerpts from the opening of each novel, notice how the tone of the third-person subjective changes to reflect the character. First from *Mrs. Bridge:*

> Her first name was India—she was never able to get used to it. It seemed to her that her parents must have been thinking of someone else when they named her. Or were they hoping for another sort of daughter? As a child she was often on the point of inquiring, but time passed, and she never did.
>
> Now and then while she was growing up the idea came to her that she could get along very nicely

without a husband, and, to the distress of her
mother and father, this idea prevailed for a number
of years after her education had been completed.
But there came a summer evening and a young lawyer named Walter Bridge . . .

—Evan S. Connell, *Mrs. Bridge*

And now from *Mr. Bridge:*

Often he thought: My life did not begin until I
knew her.

She would like to hear this, he was sure, but he
did not know how to tell her. In the extremity of
passion he cried out in a frantic voice: "I love
you!" yet even these words were unsatisfactory.
He wished for something else to say. He needed to
let her know how deeply he felt her presence while
they were lying together during the night, as well as
each morning when they awoke and in the evening
when he came home. However, he could think of
nothing appropriate.

So the years passed, they had three children and
accustomed themselves to a life together, and even-
tually Mr. Bridge decided that his wife should expect nothing more of him. After all, he was an
attorney rather than a poet; he could never pretend
to be what he was not.

—Evan S. Connell, *Mr. Bridge*

With the third-person subjective the author is able to
comment upon the character in a subtle way that
would not be possible in the first person. It is another

technique for making the character's inner life accessible to the reader.

☞*Try your hand:*

Take your original first-person narrative from the first exercise in this chapter and rewrite it in the third-person subjective. Suggest the same objective point of view that you achieved in the omniscient-narrator exercise but include more of the speaker's attitude.

TONE AND DICTION

Once you have determined the voice in which you want to write, you must begin to make some decisions about tone and about level of diction. Both are determined by purpose. Obviously your approach will vary with what you write, but if you strain for effect, the result will be awkward. When your writing sounds false, it is often because you are subconsciously attempting to sound like another writer.

You can, on the other hand, tailor your tone to your audience. Is your audience apt to be friendly? unfriendly? sympathetic? antagonistic? disinterested? uninterested? educated? knowledgeable? uninformed? Do questions of age, gender, ethnic background come into play? Are members of the audience likely to be sensitive toward language and their perceptions of your attitude? Will they be likely to misinterpret your attempts at irony or humor? Are there things you shouldn't say? things you should? Purpose provides the answers.

Tone

Tone is determined by your purpose and your desired effect. You can choose a tone that is:

aggressive	hip
angry	instructional
antagonistic	loving
authoritative	old-fashioned
committed	placating
cool	professional
consoling	romantic
descriptive	sarcastic
direct	serious
fair	understanding
formal	warm

Everyone has, at one time or another, written a letter too angry to be mailed. It is very easy to get carried away with words when passion has been aroused. A simple change in tone can make all the difference.

The two letters that follow, from A. R. Gurney's play *Love Letters,* demonstrate differences in tone. The first letter, sarcastic and angry, reflects Melissa's anger at receiving an impersonal holiday letter from an old friend, Andy. The second, warm and consoling, reflects Andy's sadness after Melissa's death. Note the ways in which Gurney uses tone: sarcasm to project Melissa's feeling of having been excluded and sincerity to project Andy's feeling of loss.

Dear Andy,

If I ever get another of those drippy Xeroxed Christmas letters from you, I think I'll invite myself out to your ducky little house for dinner, and when you're all sitting there eating terribly healthy food and discussing terribly important things and generally congratulating yourselves on all your accomplishments, I think I'll stand up on my chair, and turn around, and moon the whole fucking family!

Melissa

Dear Mrs. Gardner:

I think the first letter I ever wrote was to you, accepting an invitation for Melissa's birthday party. Now I'm writing you again about her death. I want to say a few things on paper I couldn't say at her funeral, both when I spoke, and when you and I talked afterward. As you may know, Melissa and I managed to keep in touch with each other most of our lives, primarily through letters. Even now, as I write this letter to you, I feel I'm writing it also to her.

We had a complicated relationship, she and I, all our lives. We went in very different directions. But somehow over those years, I think we managed to give something to each other. Melissa expressed all the dangerous and rebellious feelings I never dared admit to, and I like to think I gave her some sense of balance. . . .

I don't think I've ever loved anyone the way I loved her, and I know I never will again. She was at the heart of my life, and already I miss her desperately. I just wanted to say this to you and to her.

Sincerely,
Andy Ladd

— A. R. Gurney, *Love Letters*

Never feel confined to the tone of a first draft, and be wary of slipping into a tone that was not consciously chosen. Tone should always be based on a clearly articulated purpose.

You can achieve a particular tone by being particular about the words you choose. If you want to describe a place that is dark, for example, you might choose the adjective *velvety* to convey a pleasant quality. The words *menacing, dank, dreary,* and *dismal* would convey other meanings entirely. Tone is also achieved with the selection of verbs and nouns. The way those words are put together can connote a multiplicity of meanings. The words you choose are your diction, and your diction is an important element of your style.

☞*Try your hand:*

Write a letter to a business or government agency complaining about bad service or nondelivery of a product. Make your purpose "to get something off my chest" and your tone "antagonistic." Be as nasty and clever as you can, all the while maintaining an attitude of righteous indignation and high dudgeon. Polish the letter off with a sarcastic close, and read it aloud.

Now, rewrite the letter in a more sympathetic tone. Make your purpose "to get my money back" and your tone "patient." Explain what was done and not done, and end with a clear and unemotional request for action. Put the two letters side by side.

Which letter makes you feel better? Which would get action?

Diction

The words you choose constitute your diction. Diction is measured from high to low, high being the use of multisyllabic and Latinate words and low being the use of slang and vernacular. Neither is intrinsically good or bad, but each is appropriate under certain circumstances, depending upon your purpose.

The two examples below illustrate the difference between low diction and high diction.

> The girl wore a green hat and a short skirt and sheer stockings, four-and-a-half-inch French heels. She smelled of Midnight Narcissus.
>
> At the corner the man leaned close, said something in the girl's ear. She jerked away from him, giggled.
>
> "You gotta buy liquor if you take *me* home, Smiler."
>
> "Next time, baby. I'm fresh outa dough."
>
> The girl's voice got hard. "Then I tells you goodbye in the next block, handsome."
>
> "Like hell, baby," the man answered.
>
> —Raymond Chandler, "Pickup on Noon Street"

> As shadows lengthen now across the greensward, in the immortal Pelham Grenville W.'s eldritch phrase, one's thoughts turn to crepuscular things. Bats flit; bees buzz in bonnets; the millennium, yet again (you can set your clock by it), is at hand, and as the twenty-first century gets ready to welcome us with all manner of good things, let us

hope that noisy Armageddon does not intersect too
soon our "pale parabola of joy."

— Gore Vidal, preface to *At Home: Essays
1982–1988*

Chandler, writing in classic detective-story style,
talks about the "girl's" stockings and heels. He men-
tions the name of a perfume, the name of which alone
suggests its cheap bouquet. He uses "gotta" for
"have to" and "outa" for "out of." She calls him
"handsome," and he calls her "baby." Not only is
the slang appropriate in a story like "Pickup on Noon
Street," it is essential. Obviously, it would be unwise
to use diction this low in other kinds of writing.

Gore Vidal's high diction is equally specialized. It
asks a lot of the reader: that he or she know what a
"greensward" is and the definitions of the words
"eldritch" and "crepuscular." It asks that the reader
know P. G. Wodehouse by his first and middle names
and know the origins of the phrases "as shadows
lengthen now across the greensward" and "pale
parabola of joy." If the reader is ignorant of any of
these, he or she will either have to look them up or
remain ignorant.

In addition to the differences between high and low
vocabulary, words can be hot or cold, hard or soft,
inviting or off-putting. Many good writers make diction and tone choices instinctively, but the technique
can be learned. "The difference between the right
word and the almost right word," said Mark Twain,
"is the difference between lightning and a lightning
bug."

In the extracts below, notice how the words Neil

Sheehan uses to describe the battle of Ap Bac contrast the words Ann Beattie uses to describe an
adult's conceptions of the anxieties of a child. What
makes one "hard" and the other "soft"?

Normally a strafing pass by the Hueys sup-
pressed ground fire, but this time the Viet Cong
gave tit for tat. The tracer bullets from their machine guns and BARs started reaching for a "Dip-
per" as soon as one of the Hueys dove for a
strafing pass and kept reaching, swinging with the
helicopter and following it when the pilot pulled up
at the end of the run. . . . The Huey copilots also
could not see precisely where to aim their machine
guns and rockets, because they could not make out
the foxholes in the dike through the treetops and
the foliage underneath, and they were shaken at this
unexpected opposition and the bullets walloping
into their own machines.
                        — Neil Sheehan, *A Bright Shining Lie*

At night the furry fox cub in the storybook fangs
and gnaws the wire coiled in the boxspring. . . .
   At night, the child and the adult try to puzzle out
the same thing: In order to comply, does one also
need to smile? If someone is gone, are you the
same person? Will people still call? Wasn't there
an understanding that you belonged to each other?
In the future, just once, could you have a guarantee? What will there be to say if the person returns
sadder, or perhaps seeming younger or older, sur-
prised by something, changed? What if, when you

next see your lover, he has a scar on his cheek, or she has cut her beautiful curls?

— Ann Beattie, *Picturing Will*

Sheehan's diction contains the appropriate battle jargon: "strafing," "Huey," "BAR," "cross hairs," "foxholes," and "firepower." But he also is skillful enough to throw in an occasional piece of lower diction: "tit for tat" and "walloping."

Beattie's words, equally appropriate to her purpose, are from a child's world: "furry," "fangs," "storybook." Her list of nighttime questions continues in the diction of the child but takes on the anxieties of the adult. We are moved as the language begins to operate on two levels simultaneously.

There is more to the writing of good authors like these than their choice of diction. Their understanding of the human condition, their mastery of language, the elegance of their designs — all these things are beyond the scope of this chapter. The way they select their vocabulary is the lesson to be learned here.

The words you choose *are* your style. Think of words as raw materials to be manipulated with the tools explained in the chapters that follow.

☞ *Try your hand:*

Make a list of all the words you can think of that involve the senses: tastes, sounds, smells, things you touch. Try to restrict the list to nouns and verbs — no adjectives, no adverbs, no descriptive modifiers, just actions and objects.

Now make another list of all the words you can

think of that involve technology: factories, machinery, computers. Again, try to restrict the list to nouns and verbs.

Write a paragraph with each list, and compare the tones. Now, see if you can write a paragraph about electronic equipment using sensuous words and a paragraph about gardening using the technological ones.

THREE

Structure and Plot

Once upon a time there was fiction and there was nonfiction, and everyone knew which was which: Fiction told stories and nonfiction reported facts and opinions. The structure of fiction was getting from "Once upon a time" to "They lived happily ever after," and the structure of nonfiction was getting from thesis to antithesis to synthesis.

The average newspaper writer sitting down to describe a fire knew that the lead paragraph had to tell what happened, when it happened, and where it happened, and that subsequent paragraphs would tell how and why. A fiction writer sitting down to tell a story knew that it had to have a beginning, a middle, and an end, and that the characters would have to come into conflict somehow. The essayist knew that an initial assertion had to be backed up with increasingly stronger arguments, the strongest coming last.

Teachers taught writing according to these rules, and educated people knew the techniques for putting sentences and paragraphs together, as well as those for fashioning beginnings, middles, and ends. The mastery of such techniques is no longer so common.

In addition, twentieth-century writing has blurred some of the distinctions that made the forms easy to learn. For several decades now, many journalists and other factual writers have used the techniques of fiction, while fiction writers have used the techniques of nonfiction. The results of this cross-breeding are contemporary hybrid forms called, variously, nonfiction fiction, faction, metafiction, and literary journalism.

John Gardner, in his *Art of Fiction,* describes the "metafiction" of John Barth and John Fowles as fiction in which the characters know that they are characters in fiction. This self-conscious writing style has penetrated into film and television: We now see movies in which the characters know they're in movies and television in which the characters know they're on television.

Nonfiction fiction like Truman Capote's *In Cold Blood,* Norman Mailer's *Executioner's Song,* and Tom Wolfe's *Bonfire of the Vanities* further blurs the distinctions between the two forms. Superrealist fiction, like that of Mary Robison and David Leavitt, magnifies the significance of small events and turns the focus to the character's innermost thoughts and feelings. This type of fiction often needs no plot other than the seemingly unrelated events of daily life.

Nonfiction has also developed hybrid forms. Literary journalism, dubbed the "New Journalism" in 1966 by Tom Wolfe, one of its leading practitioners, violates the basic rule of journalistic objectivity. The roots of this personal style of journalism, in which the author is a participant, the first person is used, and a story line is created, go back to the 1940s and writers like A. J. Liebling, James Agee, and John Hersey. In the sixties the leading proponents of this still-young form were Joan Didion, Jane Kramer, John McPhee, and Tom Wolfe. In the seventies, Hunter Thompson's "gonzo journalism" for *Rolling Stone* brought the energy of rock and roll to the structure of nonfiction. By the nineties, the form had become another standard.

What, then, is the point of learning the traditional techniques outlined in this chapter or those in the rest of this book: using formal language, structuring sentences, and mastering so-called correct words?

The point is that even the hybrid forms depend on knowing *how* to write. You can't manipulate rules and techniques to suit your purpose if you don't understand them and are not skilled in their use.

Anyone who has to write a memo or who has labored over a business letter can benefit greatly from the rules for constructing an essay. Anyone who wants to write fiction can learn from the principles of plot. Whether you have to write nonfiction for work or school, or you want to write fiction for fame or fun, you will benefit from an understanding of the techniques of both.

THE STRUCTURE OF FICTION

"I start with a tingle," said Isak Dinesen, "a kind of a feeling of the story I will write. Then come the characters, and they take over, they make the story. But all this ends by being a plot." Plot is structure, and structure is what keeps the reader's interest — or, in Kurt Vonnegut's words, it's a way "to keep readers reading."

In his *Aspects of the Novel* E. M. Forster described the difference between a story and a plot: " 'The king died and then the queen died' is a story,'' Forster said. '' 'The king died and then the queen died of grief' is a plot.''

A story, Forster continued, is a sequence of events, one after another, that answers the question ''What happened next?'' A plot, on the other hand, engages the imagination; it makes the reader *wonder* what is going to happen next. It demands more—of both writer and reader. A good fiction writer should be able to do both: tell stories and weave plots.

Some literary forms—the detective novel, the romance novel, and most genre fiction—are particularly dependent on plot. A good screenplay, said screenwriter and novelist William Goldman, is all structure. If you are interested in writing in one of these forms, you need to develop a facility for plotting and a sure sense of structure.

If your interest is in writing literary fiction, you might think plot is unimportant. After all, much modern fiction eschews plot. ''Generally I don't even *have* a plot,'' Norman Mailer said, and John Cheever agreed: ''Plot implies narrative and a lot of crap.'' Elizabeth Hardwick tartly quipped, ''If I want a plot I'll watch *Dallas*.''

Kurt Vonnegut, however, disagrees. ''I guarantee you,'' he once said, ''that no modern story scheme, even plotlessness, will give a reader genuine satisfaction, unless one of those old-fashioned plots is smuggled in somewhere.'' Perhaps the difference is semantic. Much of the writing of Mailer, Cheever, and Hardwick seems to be plotted. If what they have put into their stories is not plot, it most certainly is some kind of structure.

Structure can be loose, it can *seem* nonexistent, but it must be there to keep the reader reading. *Something* must be there, something more than the mere recitation of incidents or the writer's insights into the human condition. What makes us keep reading, what holds the material together, is similar to a melody line in music, and anyone who has studied musical composition knows how highly structured even the simplest of melodies is.

Picasso could draw a still life; Philip Glass can compose an étude; a writer should be able to devise a plot.

Plotting

The essence of plotting is the construction of a beginning, a middle, and an end, a three-part process described by Aristotle as "complication, crisis, and resolution." It is an easy and satisfying way of telling and listening to stories. Fairy tales and fables are structured this way ("Once upon a time . . . and then one day . . . and they lived happily ever after"). So are Bible stories. So are novels like *Pride and Prejudice* and *Presumed Innocent*.

This tripartite — beginning / middle / end — structure dominated writing for centuries before experimenting writers began to shake it up. During the nineteenth and early twentieth centuries the dominant style of playwrighting was the "well-made play." Playwright and humorist George S. Kaufman defined and made fun of this type of structure when he said that "in the first act you get the hero up a tree, in the second you throw rocks at him, and in the third act you get the poor son-of-a-bitch back down.''

Plot is developed, according to Aristotle, by putting characters with opposing goals through a series of conflicts. The resolution of each conflict leads to another and greater conflict, until the largest and final conflict, the *crisis*, ensues — this is the *climax*, which brings about the *dénouement* (French for ''untying'') and the end of the story. This process is best envisioned as a long road up a bumpy hill and a sudden drop down.

In fiction, particularly in contemporary fiction, structure can vary. A single story can be narrated by different characters. The story can begin with the ending and reveal the plot through flashback, or it can begin in the middle and scramble the chronology. Whatever the arrangement, there must be some sort of structure to keep the reader reading.

''I usually begin with endings,'' said John Irving, ''with a sense of aftermath, of dust settling, of epilogue.'' For Irving, the sense of how it all comes out must come first: ''Know the story, as much of the story as you can possibly know, if not the whole story — before you commit yourself to the first paragraph.''

But you must remain flexible. According to E. M. Forster, the novelist who works forward toward the climax may alter the final event as he or she approaches it, ''indeed he probably will, indeed he probably had better, or the novel becomes tied up and tight.''

Whether you write from an outline or not, what makes the act of writing rewarding for most writers is that you discover things as you write: about the plot, the characters, the story, and writing itself.

The plot outline below, for the Edgar Allan Poe story "The Masque of the Red Death," illustrates the sequence of a classic plot: exposition, precipitating event, complication, crisis, climax, and resolution. This short story, a classic Gothic horror tale, has the elements that have become obligatory for the genre: It is tightly constructed, and the atmosphere is genuinely eerie. The story itself is reprinted on page 217 of this book. Read it now and notice how efficiently the storytelling is accomplished and how expeditiously the plot unfolds. The essential component of any narrative is propulsion: Whether the plot is fast-paced or leisurely, it must give a feeling of movement.

Poe's "Masque of the Red Death" Outlined

EXPOSITION

1. Description of the Red Death, a disease that kills instantly, leaving red stains on the body and the face, and of Prince Prospero's attempts to isolate himself from it, along with his thousand "hale and light-hearted friends."

2. Description of the night of the masked ball, the palace itself, and, especially, the black room with the blood-tinted panes.

PRECIPITATING EVENT

3. The clock strikes nine. The guests pause uneasily while the hours are sounded. The party goes on, and an hour passes.

4. The clock strikes ten. The guests wait again and then continue for another hour.
5. The clock strikes eleven. No one goes near the black room with the blood-tinted panes, but in the other rooms the party grows more wild.

COMPLICATION

6. The clock strikes midnight, and at the final stroke a figure wearing a corpselike mask appears. The mask looks like the face of someone who has died of the Red Death.

CRISIS

7. Prince Prospero orders the intruder seized, but the guests are too frightened to move.
8. The prince, brandishing a dagger, himself rushes after the intruder into the black room with the blood-tinted windows. He drops the dagger with a cry and falls to the floor.

CLIMAX

9. The guests rush in and seize the intruder, who disappears, leaving behind only the corpselike mask.

RESOLUTION

10. "And now was acknowledged the presence of the Red Death. . . . And one by one dropped the revellers in the blood-bedewed halls of their revel, and died each in the despairing posture of his fall."

Poe's structure can be easily articulated as the conflict between Prince Prospero and the Red Death. The conflict can be seen growing in intensity: The tolling of the clock grows longer hour by hour, the tension of the guests grows, and the prince's final, physical confrontation with the Red Death brings about the dénouement and the end of the story.

Outlining an already-written plot like this is much easier than outlining a plot you are planning to write: One is an academic exercise; the other is part of a creative process. Nevertheless, examining how a good old-fashioned plot functions will increase your understanding of structure.

The following exercise in plot making will help you develop a sense of structure.

☞*Try your hand:*

Devise a plot in the following manner:

1. Take a dramatic or comic event in which two people are parting at a train station or airport. One of them waves good-bye, and the other takes out a gun.
2. Working backward, create a series of conflicts that might have brought them there.
3. Decide on a precipitating event and outline the story from beginning to end.
4. Devise another version of the same story, this time starting with the climax and telling the story in flashback.
5. Now give it a happy ending.

THE STRUCTURE OF NONFICTION

Nonfiction can take many forms: history, biography, instruction, inspiration, newspaper and magazine writing, memos, and letters. Each form has its own structural requirements, but at the basis of most of them is the expository essay: a piece of writing that puts forth a proposition, defends it, and proves it. The work can be anything from a college-application essay to an op-ed piece on how the United States could have avoided war. Any piece of writing that says something is so and explains why it is so is, at basis, expository prose.

A well-constructed essay has three elements in common with a traditionally well-constructed short story: a beginning, a middle, and an end. The beginning is the thesis, the idea that is being put forth. The middle is the argument, the body of the essay, in which the thesis is defended against its antithesis. The ending is the conclusion, which restates the thesis as it has been expanded by the arguments put forth in the body. Paragraph by paragraph, there is a back-and-forth of thesis and antithesis, pro and con, argument and counterargument that is similar in rhythm to the back-and-forth of conflict and resolution in fiction.

To construct an essay in this form requires a simple, clear, logical manner of reasoning. That reasoning will provide the structure and the pace of your writing. It will move the reader from point to point. Mastering the expository essay will improve your writing, whether business letters and memos, or articles for newspapers or magazines, or books of nonfiction.

"If any man wishes to write in a clear style," wrote Goethe, "let him first be clear in his thoughts." A good outline will help you clarify your thoughts.

The Expository Essay

Outlining is essential to the success of an essay. You must know your topic and the ultimate point you wish to make. The three-part structure is more complex than merely telling them what you're going to say, saying it, and telling them that you've said it. Each paragraph should be structured to make a point, and each one should lead to the next, building your argument toward your strongest points.

Your beginning should set forth your thesis, your middle should disprove the arguments against the thesis and develop its major points, and your ending should restate the thesis or bring it to a new conclusion.

The Beginning: The Thesis

There are two basic ways to begin an essay. The first is to delay the thesis until the second or third paragraph and open, instead, by laying the groundwork, establishing a perspective, and preparing the reader for what the essay will say. You can do this by referring to a specific image or event that illustrates the thesis and drawing some conclusions about that image or event — but not yet about the thesis itself. These sentences from the opening of a December 9, 1963, column from *I. F. Stone's Weekly* illustrate how to do this. The startling thesis is the final sentence quoted here:

> There was a fairy tale quality about the inaugural and there was a fairy tale quality about the funeral rites. One half expected that when the lovely prin-

cess knelt to kiss the casket for the last time, some winged godmother would wave her wand and restore the hero whole again in a final triumph over the dark forces which had slain him. There never was such a shining pageant of a Presidency before. We watched it as children do, raptly determined to believe but knowing all the time that it wasn't really true.

Of all the Presidents, this was the first to be a Prince Charming. To watch the President at a press conference or at a private press briefing was to be delighted by his wit, his intelligence, his capacity and his youth. These made the terrible flash from Dallas incredible and painful. But perhaps the truth is that in some ways John Fitzgerald Kennedy died just in time. He died in time to be remembered as he would like to be remembered, as ever young, still victorious, struck down undefeated, with almost all the potentates and rulers of mankind, friend and foe, come to mourn at his bier.

—I. F. Stone, ''After Dallas:
We All Had a Finger on That Trigger''

The second way to open an essay is by forcefully saying exactly what's on your mind, as did Joseph Alsop in this November 25, 1963, column from the New York *Herald Tribune:*

Of all the men in public life in his time, John Fitzgerald Kennedy was the most ideally formed to lead the United States of America.

Such, at any rate, is this reporter's judgment, perhaps biased, but at any rate based on long experience and close observation, and no longer possible to suspect as self-serving.

— Joseph Alsop, "Go, Stranger, and Tell . . ."

Do you need to tell your audience your thesis right away, or can you afford to warm to your topic? Form in this case will be dictated by appropriateness.

The Middle: Details and Transitions

Somewhere in the next few paragraphs you address the antithesis: the "con" or counterarguments against which the "pro" arguments will be measured. These counterarguments offer additional perspectives and give the reader the feeling that the writer considered all alternatives before deciding on an opinion. Without these, the essay might appear to be one-sided. Depending on the issue in question there can be one con or several. They should be described quickly and disproved in a few paragraphs. Now the stage is set for the body of the argument.

The body presents the pro arguments in a logical and persuasive manner. Each separate point should have its own paragraph, and each paragraph should lead to the next. This is where the writing of an expository essay becomes a creative act: in the same way that details of plot and character can surprise when you are writing fiction, new and more powerful arguments will occur to you as you write.

Within the body of the essay details and examples will establish your credibility. Each point you make should be supported by some concrete fact or observation that makes your point seem irrefutable. In an argumentative essay on the dangers of nuclear power, each point should be backed up by facts about nuclear accidents or the dangers of terrorism. In a descriptive essay about a place, mention its sights and sounds and smells and colors. In a descriptive essay about a person, use action and dialogue. The methods for making your points are many:

- Refer to your research.
- Define terms.
- Give reasons.
- Present evidence.
- Cite specific examples.
- Point out common knowledge and common sense.
- Compare and contrast.
- Use deductive reasoning: If "a" then "b"; if "b" then "c."

Each paragraph should begin with an assertion, proceed to demonstrate it, and end with its logical conclusion: the same three-part structure, in miniature, as the essay as a whole. Sometimes, however, you may need help getting from point to point or from paragraph to paragraph. A connection that seemed clear in your mind may seem like a non sequitur on paper. The transitional words in the following list can be used to begin paragraphs or to get from sentence to sentence within a paragraph.

Transitional words and phrases

although	as a result
and	as I have said
and so	because

besides	more than that
but	moreover
consequently	most
even if	important
finally	neither
for example	nevertheless
for instance	nor
for this reason	on the
furthermore	contrary
however	on the other
in addition	hand
in fact	or
in other words	since
in particular	though
in spite of	undoubtedly
in truth	unless
indeed	what is more
meanwhile	yet
more	
specifically	

These transitional words cannot replace logical connections between thoughts, sentences, and paragraphs; they can only clarify them. However, a transition that may seem awkward will seem more logical and natural with the addition of one of these words — as the opening of this sentence illustrates.

Another common transitional device is to take a word or phrase from the previous sentence and use it to weave another point. This device will give the feeling of development and help reduce choppiness. (Look at the previous two sentences: The repetition of the word *device* is an example of this technique.)

Without these transitions your thoughts on the page can seem to wander from point to point.

The End: The Conclusion

The body of the essay should build toward the most powerful or persuasive argument, much as the crises of a story lead to the climax.

In the conclusion, the thesis is restated and expanded into a broader statement, in order to summarize the insights developed in the body of the essay. A well-constructed essay should leave the reader with a new and deeper understanding of its topic.

The following outline for Emerson's classic essay "Character" illustrates this structure. The essay itself is reprinted on page 225, and as you will see, it is remarkable for its content as well as its construction.

Emerson's essays are structured with longer paragraphs than those generally used today, and the arguments are illustrated with examples from history and literature and from the events of Emerson's society. Read it now and notice the manner and power of his reasoning.

Emerson's Essay "Character" Outlined

THESIS

¶ 1. There is a force by whose impulses we are guided, a force Emerson calls character.

CON ARGUMENTS

The next three paragraphs demonstrate this force of character in its coarsest and most common forms:

¶ 2. In political elections: It is not just what the candidate says but the way he says it that makes us choose.

¶ 3. In business dealings: Certain people inspire confidence because they have a natural probity and insight into the fabric of society.

¶ 4. In private relations: A strong mind influences a weak one.

The remainder of the essay will explain character as something deeper and more profound.

BODY OF THE ARGUMENT

The first three paragraphs of the body make three points about character:

¶ 5. Character is a natural power, like light and heat.

¶ 6. It is demonstrated by "resistance of circumstances."

¶ 7. It is proved by self-sufficiency.

The next two paragraphs describe people of character:

¶ 8. They are motivated more by spirit than by thought.

¶ 9. Their new actions are the only apologies for their old ones.

The next two paragraphs expand the definition of character by saying what is *not:*

¶ 10. It is more than a list of donations and good deeds.

¶ 11. It is more than intellect.

The next two paragraphs say what it *is:*

¶ 12. It is nature in its highest form.

¶ 13. It is an unself-conscious, innocent force.

The next four paragraphs begin to lay the groundwork for Emerson's final point: the manifestation of character in the relations between people.

¶ 14. There are persons of character so endowed with insight and virtue that we recognize them as "divine."

¶ 15. We are all born believers in the capacity for such greatness.

¶ 16. Nothing in life is so satisfying as a "profound, good understanding" between two virtuous people, each of whom is sure of himself and sure of his friend.

¶ 17. Such friends will always seek each other out.

FINAL AND STRONGEST POINT

The two penultimate paragraphs, the first of which is a seeming non sequitur, set up the final point: that

¶ 18. Most of our lives are spent ignobly, chasing "some flying scheme," but when we suddenly encounter a friend, we appreciate it.

¶ 19. Grandeur and greatness of character work in small ways.

CONCLUSION

¶ 20. If we cannot achieve great character, let us at least recognize it and honor it when we come upon it.

Paragraph 1 states the thesis by defining character and citing examples. Paragraphs 2 through 4 describe, as an antithesis, what we commonly take character to be. Paragraphs 5 through 17 form the body of the essay, building the idea of character from its simplest examples in politics and law to the idea of great character as a sign of divinity. Paragraphs 18 and 19 build the final argument: the somewhat surprising view that friendship is the true expression of character. Paragraph 20 draws the conclusion that we should value and treasure this quality in ourselves and others.

What makes Emerson's essays work is the persuasiveness of his arguments. This persuasiveness is the result of style, structure, and substance. Understanding Emerson's structure — the structure of the classic expository essay — will help you bring to any type of nonfiction writing a sure sense of how to begin, how to proceed, and how to conclude.

☞*Try your hand:*

Outline an essay in the following manner:

1. Choose a topic on which you have a strong opinion: freedom of speech, the rights of women, taxes.
2. State your thesis.
3. State at least one antithesis or counterargument and disprove it.
4. Choose five or six points that build your argument.
5. Choose your final and most persuasive point.
6. Come up with a conclusion that proves your position.

THE STRUCTURE OF NEWSPAPER AND MAGAZINE ARTICLES

The essence of a good article is a good lead, an opening that will make the reader want to read the rest. In newspaper writing it is very important that a good lead tell what happened, when, and where: "Put the story in the lead" is the old journalism-school dictum.

Pulitzer Prize–winning crime reporter Edna Buchanan, who writes about drugs and murder for *The Miami Herald,* specializes in the kind of lead that makes the reader, in her words, "spit out his coffee, clutch his chest, and say, 'My god, Martha! Did you read this?' " Here is a typical Edna Buchanan lead:

> The man she loved slapped her face. Furious, she says, she told him never, ever to do that again. "What are you going to do, kill me?" he asked, and handed her a gun. "Here, kill me," he challenged. She did.

A magazine article can have a more leisurely lead. Here is the lead from a *New Yorker* article *about* Edna Buchanan by Calvin Trillin:

> In the newsroom of *The Miami Herald,* there is some disagreement about which of Edna Buchanan's first paragraphs stands as the classic Edna lead. I line up with the fried-chicken faction. The fried-chicken story was about a rowdy ex-con named Gary Robinson, who late one Sunday night lurched drunkenly into a Church's outlet, shoved

his way to the front of the line, and ordered a three-piece box of fried chicken. Persuaded to wait his turn, he reached the counter again five or ten minutes later, only to be told that Church's had run out of fried chicken. The young woman at the counter suggested that he might like chicken nuggets instead. Robinson responded to the suggestion by slugging her in the head. That set off a chain of events that ended with Robinson's being shot dead by a security guard. Edna Buchanan covered the murder for the *Herald*—there are policemen in Miami who say that it wouldn't be a murder without her—and her story began with what the fried-chicken faction still regard as the classic Edna lead: "Gary Robinson died hungry."

And here is the actual Edna Buchanan lead:

> Gary Robinson died hungry. He wanted fried chicken, the three-piece box for $2.19. Drunk, loud and obnoxious, he pushed ahead of seven customers on line at a fast-food chicken outlet. The counter girl told him that his behavior was impolite. She calmed him down with sweet talk, and he agreed to step to the end of the line. His turn came just before closing time, just after the fried chicken ran out.
>
> He punched the counter girl so hard her ears rang, and a security guard shot him—three times.

Two different media, two different styles: The *Miami Herald* newspaper lead gives the reader the essential information, so that wherever the reader stops after the first paragraphs, he or she will have the facts. The *New Yorker* magazine lead, on the other hand, entices us to read the entire article. Both must grab, and grab quickly. The magazine lead, like the opening of a story or an essay, must also set the tone for what's to come.

The body of each type of article proceeds in the same manner as that of the expository essay: Each paragraph makes its point and leads to the next. The newspaper article puts the strongest points up front; the magazine article can do that, or it can build up to the strongest point, as an essay does. When the necessary points have been made, the article is ended. For the newspaper article, this is simply a matter of making the final point. For the magazine writer, the ending is more like the ending of a classic essay: It is what the reader will remember. A reference to the lead at the end of the piece can give the article a pleasant feeling of having come full circle. A quotation can end the article with a lift, as Gore Vidal did in this article on Tennessee Williams for *The New York Review of Books:*

I remember him best one noon in Key West during the early fifties (exact date can be determined because on every jukebox "Tennessee Waltz" was being mournfully sung by Patti Page). Each of us had finished work for the day. We met on South Beach, a real beach then. We made our way through sailors on the sand to a terraced restaurant where the Bird sat back in a chair, put his bare feet up on a railing, looked out at the bright blue sea, and, as he drank his first and only martini of the midday, said, with a great smile, "I like my life."

— Gore Vidal, "Tennessee Williams: Someone to Laugh at the Squares With"

Another device is to save the antithesis for a surprise ending, which is what Anna Quindlen did in a column about being pregnant in New York City. The article is primarily a recounting of frustrations and difficulties, but suddenly at the end she shifts her tone:

One evening rush hour during my eighth month I was waiting for a train at Columbus Circle. The loudspeaker was crackling unintelligibly and ominously and there were as many people on the platform as currently live in Santa Barbara, Calif. Suddenly I had the dreadful feeling that I was being surrounded. "To get mugged at a time like this," I thought ruefully. "And this being New York, they'll probably try to take the baby, too." But as I looked around I saw that the people surrounding me were four women, some armed with shopping bags. "You need protection," one said, and being New Yorkers, they ignored the fact that they did not know each other and joined forces to form a kind of phalanx around me, not unlike those that offensive linemen build around a quarterback.

When the train arrived and the doors opened, they moved forward, with purpose, and I was swept inside, not the least bit bruised. "Looks like a boy," one said with a grin, and as the train began to move, we all grabbed the silver overhead handles and turned away from one another.

— Anna Quindlen, "Pregnant in New York"

☞*Try your hand:*

Choose an event from your life and report it first as a news item: in the third-person objective, telling what happened, when it happened, and where it happened.

Then tell it as a magazine article, in the first person, reflecting as well on what the event meant to you.

THE STRUCTURE OF THE MEMO
AND THE LETTER

The basic principles of nonfiction writing can help you in your business correspondence. Letters and memos should be structured so that they are simple, clear, and to the point, although a certain formality may be necessary to project an appropriate, business-like manner.

Many memos and business letters are painful to read because they are so badly written. Although there may be mistakes in grammar or spelling, usually the real problem is that there is no structure to develop the thought. The structure of the expository essay is best here: a thesis in the first paragraph; any antitheses dispatched in the second paragraph; the body of the argument in the subsequent paragraphs; and a conclusion in the final paragraph.

The Memo

The following guidelines will help you structure a memo:

- Use a clear subject line.
- State your purpose in the first paragraph.
- Summarize any potential objections.
- Keep the paragraphs short.
- Use subheads between paragraph groups.
- Use bulleted and numbered lists.
- Request action.

Use a clear subject line.

The words that follow the "Re:" should state the subject of the memo succinctly. Whoever will read your memo is undoubtedly busy. Your goal in composing a memo, therefore, should be to write something with a clearly stated purpose that can be quickly grasped.

The subject line should let the reader know immediately whether this particular memo requires immediate attention or can wait. "Re: Promotion for John Smith" or "Re: Tenth-Floor Computer Equipment" tells the reader exactly what the memo will be about and suggests its degree of urgency.

State your purpose in the first paragraph.

The first paragraph should state the request or the recommendation in positive and unapologetic terms. Something as simple as "In his three years with the company, John Smith has proved himself an invaluable asset" or "I would like to requisition additional computer equipment for the tenth floor" states the case simply and without undue campaigning.

Your proposal may or may not be accepted, but your tone of voice should project a sense of confidence in what you are proposing.

Summarize any potential objections.

If you anticipate that there will be objections to the request or recommendation, they should be covered in the second paragraph, in the same manner that antitheses are dispatched in the second paragraph of the expository essay:

> I understand the reasons for limiting the number of additional PCs being purchased at the present time, but two more units on the tenth floor will improve efficiency and cut costs.

Keep the paragraphs short.

One-sentence paragraphs are fine in business correspondence. Anything longer than three sentences may look imposing and discourage the reader from reading or cooperating. Chattiness and long-windedness will only annoy.

Use subheads between paragraph groups.

If the material to be covered is complex, break it into several small paragraphs and use subheads between the paragraph groups. The subheads should be like additional subject lines: They should state exactly what will be covered in the next few paragraphs.

Don't be afraid that the subheads and the paragraphs that follow will be repetitive. The convenience of the reader is what you're aiming for. Underline the subhead and use double spacing before or after.

If, on the other hand, you choose to use the bells and whistles of your computer program, beware of overwhelming your message with too many different typefaces and sizes.

Use bulleted and numbered lists.

If a list is longer than three items, consider typing it as a bulleted list. This can be done by indenting and using an asterisk or the letter *o*. If the items carry over to a second line, indent either the first line or the subsequent lines.

Use a numbered rather than a bulleted list only when the numerical order of the items mentioned is important. Otherwise the numbers will be distracting.

Request action.

Unless you are writing a strictly informational memo, you should end with a request for action from the person you are addressing. The request should leave the reader with a clear understanding of how you would like him or her to proceed.

The following memo strikes an appropriate tone and doesn't waste the reader's time.

Memorandum

To: Peter Lowell
From: Toria Krantz
Date: November 30, 1990
Re: Tenth-floor Computer Equipment

I would like to requisition additional computer equipment for the tenth floor.

I understand the reasons for limiting the number of additional PCs being purchased at the present time, but two more units on the tenth floor will improve efficiency and cut costs.

At present, we have one PC for general use and a failing laptop in my office. These serve a staff of eight people who use them for correspondence, fact-checking, and, increasingly, editing.

Integrating more computers into our department will mean we can save a step in the editing process and greatly increase the productivity of the department.

Please let me know whether we will be able to add the equipment.

☞*Try your hand:*

Outline a memo to show that you need to increase staff.

1. State your purpose clearly in the subject line and opening paragraph.
2. Cover any possible objections in the second paragraph.
3. Give good, compelling reasons in subsequent paragraphs, using bulleted or numbered lists if necessary.
4. End with a request for action.

The Business Letter

Similar principles hold for business letters: The first paragraph should state the purpose and the paragraphs should be kept short. More and more business letters include a subject line. Bulleted and numbered lists and subheads can be used to break up blocks of text on the page. In sales and marketing letters, the first paragraph, known as the "grabber," should resemble a good newspaper lead.

Letters should follow these five guidelines:

- Get to the point.
- Be brief.
- Say what you mean.
- Be positive.
- Be natural.

Get to the point.

Like a good memo and a good newspaper article, a good business letter will quickly state its purpose. "I am writing to inquire as to the availability of freelance work." "I wish to register a complaint about damage done to my property by your employees."

Be brief.

Say what you have to say and then stop.

Say what you mean.

Beware of falling into the style of a form letter. Say what's on your mind as succinctly as you can.

Be positive.

Never mail the letter that merely gets things off your chest. A tone of excessive complaint or sarcasm will not get you what you want, which is action.

State your complaints in a subsequent paragraph, and use the balance of the letter to say what you would like done — in simple, positive language that is free from sarcasm or bitterness.

Remember that a bitter letter is apt to get "lost" on someone's desk. Your goal should be to get someone to pay attention and *want* to help.

Be natural.

Although formal language is appropriate in many situations, it is important to feel comfortable with the words used in any letter you sign. For more on the use of formal and informal language in such letters, see Chapter Four.

Over 275 examples of commonly used types of letters can be found in the *Random House Book of Contemporary Business Letters,* edited by Stephen P. Elliott. Here is a sample business letter from Elliott's book, a response to a false credit report:

Company Name
Address
City, State, Zip

Date

Ms. Leila Foxx
Equitable Credit Check
6789 Loyola Drive
San Jose, CA 95125

Dear Ms. Foxx:

As I stated on the phone, the information in your files relating to our mortgage payment history is erroneous. As you can see from the attached statements provided by Howland Savings Bank, the holder of our mortgage, we have never been notified of foreclosure proceedings, as stipulated in your file. In fact, our company's payment record is exemplary, as you can clearly see.

I will look forward to seeing a new synopsis of our company, indicating that this grossly false statement has been corrected, and to seeing, as you promised on the phone, copies of letters detailing the correct information to all those who have made inquiries about our credit standing.

Sincerely,
Georgia T. Kroner
Vice President, Finance

Attachments

As you can see, the letter gets to the point, is brief, says what needs to be said, is positive, and is natural. It communicates the seriousness of the situation and requests action. It is, in short, good writing—in a business letter.

☞ *Try your hand:*

Take the letter of complaint from the exercise in tone in the previous chapter (page 28). Rewrite it, using the guidelines described in this chapter:

• Get to the point.
• Be brief.

- Say what you mean.
- Be positive.
- Be natural.

End your letter with a clear request for action.

FOUR

Formal and Familiar

There is a recognizably American style of writing: It is plain, straightforward, and concrete. It is neither the slang of the street nor the loftiness of Henry James. It is the prose of our newspapers and magazines, of Mark Twain and Ernest Hemingway. It is no-nonsense and not highfalutin. It is direct and to the point.

This does not mean that familiar speech cannot be eloquent or that American speech is never formal. When we hear the speeches of John F. Kennedy or the sermons of Martin Luther King, Jr., we recognize their cadences as powerful and moving, and as different from the plain style of everyday speech and writing.

What we are recognizing is the difference between two styles—the formal and the familiar—a difference that goes back to the eighteenth-century distinction between ''plain'' and ''gaudy'' prose, and even further back, to the ancient Greek distinction between ''vulgar,'' ''plain,'' ''middle,'' and ''grand'' speech. The formal may have grown unpopular, but much in it can be admired and used. Understanding the features of both formal and familiar styles can help you enrich your own writing.

* * *

In 1776 Thomas Paine published a pamphlet entitled "Common Sense," which advocated separation from England. Written primarily in what was then considered the familiar style, the pamphlet sold over 120,000 copies in its first three months and over 400,000 copies by the end of the Revolutionary War, which represents 13 percent of the population of 3 million. (If a book sold to 13 percent of the American population today, it would sell over 30 million copies.) "Common Sense" changed the opinions of tens of thousands of Americans, and altered the course of history. What made Paine's words so persuasive?

The content, of course, had much to do with the impact. Paine's words were deeply felt, and they spoke to the concerns of the people who were living in a volatile society. But others shared his passion, and others had advocated revolution. Something about Paine's style made his words especially powerful then; that something still makes them powerful today.

"In the following pages I offer nothing more than simple facts, plain arguments, and common sense," the pamphlet begins. Paine asks the reader to divest himself of "prejudice and prepossession" and allow his feelings to "determine for themselves." Some of his words may sound formal today, but in 1776, Paine's style was considered familiar even to the point of being vulgar:

> But Britain is the parent country, say some. Then more the shame upon her conduct. Even brutes do not devour their young, nor savages make war upon their families.

The seventeenth-century translators of the King James Bible had used the formal style to great effect, and the poetry and majesty of their words had kept the style alive in contemporary sermons and the speeches of politicians. But by the beginning of the eighteenth century, writers began to rebel against such formality and to write more conversationally. What Paine did in "Common Sense," however, was revolutionary: He combined the two styles.

As "Common Sense" moves on from its first sentences, Paine's diction begins to shift toward the formal. The *hath*s increase, the sentences lengthen, and there are more periodic sentences, subordinate clauses, and repetition — the hallmarks of the formal style. Driving it all is a forward-moving energy, a sure and steady progression to a climax. Having won the reader over with his commonsense, familiar manner, Paine shifts to the lofty, grand, and elevated for his closing:

> O! ye that love mankind! Ye that dare oppose, not only the tyranny, but the tyrant, stand forth! Every spot of the old world is overrun with oppression. Freedom hath been hunted round the globe. Asia, and Africa, have long expelled her. Europe regards her like a stranger, and England hath given her warning to depart. O receive the fugitive, and prepare in time an asylum for mankind.

This combination of formal and informal is a technique that preachers and politicians have used through the ages and one that you can use in your own writing to powerful effect.

FORMAL STYLE

We automatically use different kinds of formal style when we are writing a job application, a letter to an editor or congressperson, or a letter of condolence; generally we do so with a certain awkwardness because the formal as a means of personal expression hardly exists in our own time. It is not taught in schools; it is not ordinarily seen in newspapers or magazines. It is rarely spoken on television. It is heard only in sermons and in occasional political speeches, particularly those of politicians whose oratory is still rich with biblical cadences and allusions.

Shakespeare used the formal effortlessly, as did Donne and Milton, Charles Dickens and Abraham Lincoln. Even Mark Twain used it on occasion. In the twentieth century, the political speeches of Franklin Delano Roosevelt, Winston Churchill, and John F. Kennedy all gained a certain majesty from it, and the speeches of Martin Luther King, Jr., used the formal techniques of sermon oratory, which were derived directly from the style of the King James Bible.

These techniques can be employed to greater or lesser degrees in much that you write, adding power and richness to your natural manner of expression. They are especially useful when solemnity or a feeling of classicity or tradition are appropriate. The hallmarks of formal style are:

• periodic and loose sentences
• parallelism, repetition, and contraction
• metaphor and comparison

• Latinate language and multisyllabic words
• allusions

These techniques are merely tools. Combining formal techniques with your natural voice will improve your style dramatically.

The goal is simple: *to use language more effectively.*

PERIODIC AND LOOSE SENTENCES

A sentence can be as short as a single verb or as long as the writer can keep the reader's attention. A periodic sentence is one that, separated by subordinate clauses and leaving the completion of its main clause to the end, creates a feeling of suspense. (That was a periodic sentence.)

A loose sentence has its subject and verb together, preceded or followed by subordinate clauses that modify the main clause. Sentences like these are best used in descriptions of complicated matters or when the accrual of clauses or images will be effective.

Unlike these longer sentences, simple sentences suggest informality and directness. Ernest Hemingway's writing is known for them: "It is a silent procession. Nobody even grunts. It is all they can do to keep moving." Short sentences suggest urgency. They hold the attention. They are appropriate in business memos, advertising copy, and essays or articles aimed at audiences unfamiliar with the subject matter. They are also appropriate in fiction or nonfiction that describes quick action or powerful emotions being held in check.

Longer sentences must be constructed with great care or the reader will get lost on the way to the period. Well controlled, they can provide a dramatic narrative drive. One of the most powerful examples of a loose sentence is the ending of the Gettysburg Address:

> It is rather for us to be here dedicated to the great task remaining before us, — * that from these honored dead we take increased devotion to that cause to which they gave the last full measure of devotion; that we here highly resolve that these dead shall not have died in vain; that this nation, under God, shall have a new birth of freedom; and that government of the people, by the people, and for the people shall not perish from the earth.

A sentence like this has an architecture that is even more apparent when it is read out loud. Reduced to several short sentences and translated into contemporary familiar style, the passage loses its power:

> On the other hand, we should be dedicated to this great task here. We should pray for the soldiers who died here and hope that they didn't die in vain. We should promise to try to protect freedom. Our

*Note the comma-dash combination, which has disappeared from common usage, along with the colon-dash (:—) and period-dash (.—) combinations, all of which can be found throughout the Constitution and the Declaration of Independence.

government should be ours, and we should be in charge of it. It should help us, too. We should make sure that it's always here.

A loose sentence combines several complex thoughts into one long sentence, separating the components with commas and semicolons. It often has a participial phrase at the beginning:

• Singing its merry little song, the bluebird flew away.

or in the middle:

• The little bluebird, singing its merry song, flew away.

Contemporary writers like William F. Buckley, Jr., and Gore Vidal use these sentences to show off their literary dexterity and test the reader's ability to follow. This periodic sentence begins Vidal's essay on the early-twentieth-century American writer Logan Pearsall Smith:

Should the human race survive the twentieth of those wondrous centuries since shepherds quaked at the sight of God's birth in a Middle Eastern stable (all in all, a bad career move), our century will be noted more for what we managed to lose along the way than for what we acquired.
                              —Gore Vidal, "Logan Pearsall Smith Loves
                                                   the Adverb"

Parsing this sentence down to its subject, its predicate, and its objects reduces it to:

• Our century will be noted for what we lost.

Vidal's sentences wander deliberately. They are filled with obscure allusions and literary puns. The reader is expected to get the allusions and chuckle at the puns. His sentences test the reader's concentration and willingness to persevere. If you get lost, Vidal seems to be saying, go read something else.

Here is an elegant sentence by the subject of Vidal's admiration, Logan Pearsall Smith himself, from his classic collection of short essays, *Trivia:*

> Sitting for hours in the shade of an apple tree, near the garden-hives, and under the aerial thoroughfares of those honey-merchants,—sometimes when the noonday heat is loud with their minute industry, or when they fall in crowds out of the late sun to their night-long labours,—I have sought instruction from the Bees, and tried to appropriate to myself the old industrious lesson.
>
> —Logan Pearsall Smith, ''The Busy Bees''

Parsed down to its subject and verb, the sentence reads:

• I have sought instruction and tried.

Contemporary writers use long sentences to establish a specific tone and style. Here is one that is both loose and periodic, from Vladimir Nabokov's memoir, *Speak, Memory*. The labyrinthine quality of the sentence helps Nabokov weave his spell:

> While politely discussing with him my father's sudden journey to town, I registered simultaneously and with equal clarity not only his wilting flowers, his flowing tie and the blackheads on the fleshy volutes of his nostrils, but also the dull little voice of a cuckoo coming from afar, and the flash of a Queen of Spain settling on the road, and the remembered impression of the pictures (enlarged agricultural pests and bearded Russian writers) in the well-aerated classrooms of the village school which I had once or twice visited; and—to continue a tabulation that hardly does justice to the ethereal simplicity of the whole process—the throb of some utterly irrelevant recollection (a pedometer I had lost) was released from a neighboring brain cell, and the savor of the grass stalk I was chewing mingled with the cuckoo's note and the fritillary's takeoff, and all the while I was richly, serenely aware of my own manifold awareness.
>
> —Vladimir Nabokov, *Speak, Memory*

Within this sentence there are three independent clauses. Parsed down to their subjects and predicates, they are:

- I registered his flowers, his tie, and the blackheads, the voice, the flash, and the impression.
- The throb was released.
- The savor mingled.
- I was aware of my awareness.

Lengthy sentences needn't be coupled with high diction. Sometimes an effect of time or weight can be created. In the following sentence, the opening of her short story "Tepeyac," author Sandra Cisneros gives a panoramic view of a small Mexican town. Form matches content: The long list of subordinate clauses and the length of the sentence itself help to give the feeling of the length of the day:

When the sky of Tepeyac opens its first thin stars and the dark comes down in an ink of Japanese blue above the bell towers of La Basílica de Nuestra Señora, above the plaza photographers and their souvenir backdrops of La Virgen de Guadalupe, above the balloon vendors and their balloons wearing paper hats, above the red-canopied thrones of the shoeshine stands, above the wooden booths of the women frying lunch in vats of oil, above the *tlapaleria* on the corner of Misterios and Cinco de Mayo, when the photographers have toted up their tripods and big box cameras, have rolled away the wooden ponies I don't know where, when the balloon men have sold all but the ugliest balloons and herded the last few home, when the shoeshine men have grown tired of squatting on their little wooden boxes, and the women frying lunch have finished packing dishes, tablecloth, pots, in the big straw basket in which they came, then Abuelito tells the boy with dusty hair, *Arturo, we are closed,* and in crooked shoes and purple elbows Arturo pulls down with a pole the corrugated metal curtains — first the one on Misterios, then the other on Cinco

de Mayo—like an eyelid over each door, before
Abuelito tells him that he can go.

—Sandra Cisneros, "Tepeyac"

Periodic and loose sentences can be extremely effective. But used without sufficient precision, they
can make your prose labored, pretentious, and dull. If
you find yourself using too many short choppy sentences, try tying them together with subordinate
clauses. Conversely, if you find yourself using long
sentences with many clauses and semicolons, you can
try breaking them up. You needn't choose long sentences or short sentences as your exclusive style. Develop a taste for both and a sense of when each is
effective.

☞*Try your hand:*
Make a list of what you did when you woke up:
I opened my eyes.
I turned off the alarm.
I got out of bed, etc.
Now make that list into a periodic sentence:
Having opened my eyes and shut off the alarm, I
got out of bed . . .
Now make a list of your evening activities and turn
those into a periodic sentence.

PARALLELISM, REPETITION, AND
CONTRACTION

Much of the power of formal prose comes from the
repetition of words and phrases and the connections

made between them. Balance can be achieved by putting together two members of a single pair:

• ladies and gentlemen

two pairs of twin items:

• lovely ladies and kind gentlemen

two compounds of three elements:

• ladies of dubious virtue, gentlemen of low repute

or two compounds of four or more elements:

• lovely ladies of dubious virtue, kind gentlemen of low repute

This balance in construction is known as parallelism.

Dozens of these ancient patterns of repetition and parallelism—and similar patterns of contraction—were identified by nineteenth-century teachers of rhetoric. These patterns, called figures of speech or "tropes," became the principles of rhetoric upon which formal oratory and writing were based. These same techniques can still be used effectively.

You can, for example, repeat or add a word for emphasis or for rhythm:

• Verily, verily, I say unto you.
• Thy rod and thy staff they comfort me.

The second "verily," the second "thy," and the word "they" could be deleted—with a loss of poetry but not of meaning.

You can repeat conjunctions in close succession to create a "piling up" of elements:

• apples and oranges and peaches and pears

Or you can leave out the conjunctions and separate the list with commas to imply fast, expeditious movement:

• I came, I saw, I conquered.

Repeating words at the beginning of two or more successive clauses or sentences can be a dramatic means of emphasis:

• We cannot dedicate—we cannot consecrate—we cannot hallow this ground.

Do the same thing at the end of a sentence for a more matter-of-fact but still-strong result:

• I should do Brutus wrong, and Cassius wrong.

Or combine the two:

• It was the best of times, it was the worst of times . . .

Similarly, you can leave out any word or phrase in the sentence to avoid the repetition of a parallel element:

• In the one we must admire the man; in the other the work.

This common kind of contraction is known as ellipsis.

Many of these techniques have regularly been used in the speeches of American presidents, as in this moral lesson from Woodrow Wilson:

> There has been something crude and heartless and unfeeling in our haste to be great. Our thought has been "Let every man look out for himself; let every generation look out for itself," while we reared giant machinery which made it impossible that any but those who stood at the levers of control should have any chance to look out for themselves.

Peggy Noonan, who wrote speeches for Ronald Reagan and George Bush, complained that the quality of modern speeches has declined because "we as a nation no longer learn the rhythms of public utterance from Shakespeare and the Bible." She employed for George Bush a new, less formal kind of ellipsis: She left out the pronouns at the beginning of his sentences, giving his speeches a clipped, businesslike tone:

> Worked in the oil business and then started our own. . . . Moved from the shotgun to a duplex apartment to a house. And lived the dream . . . school football on Friday nights, Little League, neighborhood barbecue.

The speeches of John Kennedy, on the other hand, made memorable use of repetition and other techniques of formal diction:

- Ask not what your country can do for you — ask what you can do for your country.
- Peace in space will help us naught once peace on earth is gone.

The most powerful use of formal style in recent history was the "I Have a Dream" speech by Martin Luther King, Jr., from the 1963 March on Washington. Like Thomas Paine's "Common Sense," this speech changed the way people viewed the world. And like "Common Sense," it combined the formal with the familiar. It also continued the connection between formal style and the sermon oratory. Notice the climax of repetitions at the beginnings of the paragraphs:

I have a dream that one day this nation will rise up and live out the true meaning of its creed: "We hold these truths to be self-evident; that all men are created equal."

I have a dream that one day on the red hills of Georgia the sons of former slaves and the sons of former slave-owners will be able to sit down together at the table of brotherhood.

I have a dream that one day even the state of Mississippi, a desert state sweltering with the heat of injustice and oppression, will be transformed into an oasis of freedom and justice.

I have a dream that my four little children will

one day live in a nation where they will not be judged by the color of their skin but by the content of their character.

I have a dream today.

This is the first of several climaxes, with a progression of initial repetitions to another climax:

I have a dream that the state of Alabama, whose governor's lips are presently dripping with the words of interposition and nullification, will be transformed into a situation where little black boys and black girls will be able to join hands with little white boys and white girls and walk together as sisters and brothers.

I have a dream today.

After this comes another climax that uses repetition and parallelism to echo the images and language of the Bible:

I have a dream that one day every valley shall be exalted, every hill shall be made low, the rough place will be made plain, and the crooked places will be made straight, and the glory of the Lord shall be revealed, and all the flesh shall see it together.

Devices like these are most useful when you are writing with strong emotion. They give form to passion without softening the message. In 1936 journalist Dorothy Thompson began filing a series of reports from Germany on the encroaching Nazi menace. This

one, from February 18, 1938, makes chilling use of
the repetition of an initial phrase:

> Write it down. On Saturday, February 12, 1938,
> Germany won the world war, and dictated, in Berch-
> tesgaden, a peace treaty to make the Treaty of Ver-
> sailles look like one of the greatest humane docu-
> ments of the ages.
>
> Write it down. On Saturday, February 12, 1938,
> Naziism started on the march across all of Europe
> east of the Rhine.
>
> Write it down that the world revolution began in
> earnest—and perhaps the world war.
>
> Write it down that what not even the leaders of
> the German army could stomach—they protested,
> they resigned, they lost their posts—so-called
> Christian and democratic civilization accepted,
> without risking one drop of brave blood.
>
> Write it down that the democratic world broke
> its promises and its oath, and capitulated, not
> before strength, but before terrible weakness,
> armed only with ruthlessness and audacity.
>
> What happened?

The effect that Thompson achieves in that last question by switching from the formal to the familiar is
similar to the power that Thomas Paine achieved by
switching from familiar to formal. A shift in tone at
the right moment can take the reader by surprise and
make the point more dramatically.

Another impassioned use of rhetoric comes from a
1989 speech by AIDS activist Vito Russo, at the State

Capitol in Albany, New York. Russo uses the repetition of a final phrase to contrast the classical rhythm and his angry, vernacular diction:

The media tells people they don't *have* to care, because the citizens who really matter are in no danger. Twice, three times, maybe four times, *The New York Times* has published editorials saying, ''Don't panic yet over AIDS'' — it still hasn't entered the general population, and, until it does, we don't have to give a shit.

And the days and the months and the years go by, and they don't spend those days and nights and months and years trying to figure out how to get ahold of the latest experimental drug, and which dose to take, and in what combination with what other drugs, and where do you get it, and for how much money — because it isn't happening to them, so they don't give a shit. . . .

They don't spend their waking hours going from one hospital to another, watching the people they love die slowly of bigotry and neglect — because it isn't happening to them, so they don't give a shit.

They haven't been to two funerals a week for the past three or four or five years, so they don't give a shit.

It's not happening to *them*.

☞*Try your hand:*
Make a list of complaints about bad service from your landlord or from a telephone, utility, or cable company. Repeat a phrase at the beginning:

I did not receive heat on January 1. I did not receive heat on January 5. I did not receive heat on January 7.

Repeat a phrase at the end:

On January 11 I had no phone service. On January 12 I had no phone service. On January 15 I had no phone service.

Repeat a conjunction:

My cable was out on February 2 and February 4 and February 5 and February 7.

Now make a list of your own and go after the scoundrels.

METAPHOR AND COMPARISON

A comparison likens one object to a similar object: "She acts just like her mother." It becomes a simile when the two objects being compared are by nature dissimilar: "She acts *like* a mother hen." The simile creates the connection between them, usually with the conjunctions "like" and "as." Comparisons and similes are part of familiar style; we use them in our everyday speech.

A comparison becomes a metaphor when the two objects are equated and not compared: "She is the mother of us all" instead of "She is like a mother to us." Actual maternity is beside the point; figurative motherhood is being invoked, as it is in "the mother of all battles." Aristotle described metaphor as the "intuitive perception of the similarity in dissimilars." You perceive one thing *as* another.

There are other figures of comparison that are useful: Antithesis places one part of a sentence in direct contrast to another. The opening of Dickens's *Tale of Two Cities*, previously quoted, is an example of antithesis:

> It was the best of times, it was the worst of times, it was the age of wisdom, it was the age of foolishness, it was the epoch of belief, it was the epoch of incredulity, it was the season of Light, it was the season of Darkness, it was the spring of hope, it was the winter of despair, we had everything before us, we had nothing before us, we were all going direct to heaven, we were all going direct the other way—in short, the period was so far like the present period . . .
> —Charles Dickens, *A Tale of Two Cities*

You can use the name of one object or concept for that of another: "From the cradle to the grave" really means "from birth to death." "The crown" and "the throne" are often used for "the king" or "the queen."

Personification is the representation of an object or an imaginary, absent, or deceased person as alive. Again, the translators of the King James Bible used this figure of speech frequently to great effect:

• Tremble, thou earth, at the presence of the Lord, at the presence of the God of Jacob.

An especially dramatic device is to address an absent or dead person or a personified abstraction as if he or she were there:

- O my son Absalom, my son, my son, Absalom! would God I had died for thee, O Absalom, my son, my son!

Similes and metaphors must be used with care. They can easily sound affected or self-conscious or be unwisely mixed. No gaffe exposes a writer to ridicule more than the mixed metaphor, often a cliché gone askew:

- Keep an ear to the grindstone.
- Don't look a gift horse in the eye.
- You're treading on thin ground.

One of the most famous of mixed metaphors is an outburst in the House of Lords, attributed to the Irish politician Sir Boyle Roche:

Mr. Speaker, I smell a rat! I see it floating in the air; and if it is not nipped in the bud, it will burst forth into a terrible conflagration that will deluge the world!

As long as there are politicians seeking to inspire, metaphors and similes will be with us. Winston Churchill said: ''How infinite is the debt owed to metaphors by politicians who want to speak strongly but are not sure what they are going to say.'' The final four sentences from Tom Paine's ''Common Sense,'' which began this chapter, constitute one extended metaphor: freedom as the personification of an American immigrant.

Freedom hath been hunted round the globe. Asia, and Africa, have long expelled her. Europe regards her like a stranger, and England hath given her warning to depart. O receive the fugitive, and prepare in time an asylum for mankind.

And, of course, there is the simile that some say won an election—George Bush's simile at the end of his acceptance speech during the 1988 Republican National Convention:

This is America: the Knights of Columbus, the Grange, Hadassah, the Disabled American Veterans, the Order of Ahepa, the Business and Professional Women of America, the union hall, the Bible study group, LULAC, Holy Name—a brilliant diversity spread like stars, like a thousand points of light in a broad and peaceful sky.

☞*Try your hand:*
Describe a series of events that took place at a family gathering.
1. Describe them simply, without characterizing them.
2. Compare the events to those on another family occasion.
3. Use a simile to describe the event.
4. Come up with a metaphor for the occasion.
5. Now use antithesis and personification.

Now, mix a few metaphors—just for fun.

LATINATE LANGUAGE AND
MULTISYLLABIC WORDS

The language that we call English began as a dialect of Ancient Germanic, with the invasion of Britain by three tribes from northern Germany—the Angles, the Saxons, and the Jutes—in the fifth and sixth centuries A.D. This Anglo-Saxon language gave us many of our basic everyday words, like *word, house, dog,* and *laughter.*

English came into contact with Latin with the introduction of Christianity into England in the early Middle Ages, but Latin was not initially a source for new English words. The Norman invasion changed that—and changed the vocabulary of English forever. French words were borrowed into the language, so that we had French-derived words like *royal* and *beef* existing alongside the native English *kingly* and *cow.* The developing fields of science, medicine, law, and literature used Latin and French rather than English, bringing in new sets of words. Latinate suffixes flooded the language: abstract adjectives ending in *-able, -ible, -ous, -ive, -ent,* and *-al;* abstract verbs ending in *-ize;* and abstract nouns ending in *-ation* and *-ism.*

To this day, Anglo-Saxon-derived words tend to seem earthy and concrete, while Latin-derived words often seem lofty and abstract, with French-derived words falling somewhere in the middle. The following table is culled from the examples of literary historian Albert C. Baugh:

Anglo-Saxon	French	Latin
rise	mount	ascend
ask	question	interrogate
goodness	virtue	probity
fast	firm	secure
fire	flame	conflagration
fear	terror	trepidation
time	age	epoch

As you can see, using Latin words would give your writing a more formal tone than the Anglo-Saxon ones would. In the proper context, that tone is appropriate; in the wrong context, it can make you sound pompous or foolish.

Like Latinate vocabulary, multisyllabic words are often used for formal effect. They can be pompous or silly, but they can also, in the words of linguist Otto Jespersen, "heighten the tone, and add dignity, even majesty to the structure of the sentence." The longer word, Jespersen suggested, "takes up more time. Instead of hurrying the reader or listener on to the next idea, it allows his mind to dwell for a longer time upon the same idea; it gives time for his reflexion to be deeper and especially for his emotion to be stronger."

In *Possession,* A. S. Byatt's novel about two academics researching a love affair between two Victorian poets, she uses the characters' multisyllabic diction to illustrate their growing love for each other, to point it up ironically, and to contrast their emotions with their intellectualizations:

> They were children of a time and culture that mistrusted love, "in love," romantic love, romance *in toto,* and which nevertheless in revenge proliferated sexual language, linguistic sexuality, analysis, dissection, deconstruction, exposure. They were theoretically knowing: they knew about phallocracy and penisneid, punctuation, puncturing and penetration, about polymorphous and polysemous perversity, orality, good and bad breasts, clitoral tumescence, vesicle persecution, the fluids, the solids, the metaphors for these, the systems of desire and damage, infantile greed and oppression and transgression, the iconography of the cervix and the imagery of the expanding and contracting Body, desired, attacked, consumed, feared.
>
> —A. S. Byatt, *Possession*

ALLUSION

Another aspect of formal style is the use of classical, biblical, or literary allusions. This gives a legitimate air of sophistication, and it is a legitimate source of wit—under the right circumstances. Used inappropriately, this technique risks alienating the reader. Use allusions to put your words into a context, when you are certain that the context will be understood and appreciated.

T. S. Eliot's poetry is filled with allusions to Shakespeare, Dante, the Bible, Vergil, Ovid, and

Sappho—to mention but a few. According to Eliot's own notes, these lines from "The Waste Land" refer to lines from Ezekiel and Ecclesiastes XII:

> What are the roots that clutch, what branches grow
> Out of this stony rubbish? Son of man,
> You cannot say, or guess, for you know only
> A heap of broken images, where the sun beats,
> And the dead tree gives no shelter, the cricket no
>   relief,
> And the dry stone no sound of water.
> —T. S. Eliot, "The Waste Land"

The line alluded to from Ezekiel is:

> And he said to me, "Son of man, stand upon your feet, and I will speak with you."
> —Ezekiel II, i

The other allusion is more obscure:

> They are afraid also of what is high, and terrors are in the way; the almond tree blossoms, the grasshopper drags itself along and desire fails . . .
> —Ecclesiastes XII, v

The use of allusion is not confined to references to classical or older writings. Allusions can be made to almost any cultural or historical phenomenon. Contemporary writers often make allusions to recent fiction, popular music, television programs, and even advertising slogans. F. Scott Fitzgerald used allusions to the popular music of his day to do more than merely provide atmosphere. Notice how the lyrics to "The Sheik of Araby" in the following excerpt from *The Great Gatsby* not only paint the period but also give a sense of Gatsby's true desire in wanting to live close to Daisy:

When Jordan Baker had finished telling all this we had left the Plaza for half an hour and were driving in a victoria through Central Park. The sun had gone down behind the tall apartments of the movie stars in the West Fifties, and the clear voices of little girls, already like crickets on the grass, rose through the hot twilight:

"I'm the Sheik of Araby.
Your love belongs to me.
At night when you're asleep
Into your bed I'll creep—"

"It was a strange coincidence," I said.

"It wasn't a coincidence at all."

"Why not?"

"Gatsby bought that house so that Daisy would be just across the bay."

Then it had not been merely the stars to which he had aspired on that June night. He came alive to me, delivered suddenly from the womb of his purposeless splendor.

—F. Scott Fitzgerald, *The Great Gatsby*

Humor is especially dependent on allusion. In the following excerpt from Dave Barry's tongue-in-cheek history of the United States, note how Barry mixes allusions to history and popular culture as he summarizes the Civil War:

Brother fought against brother, unless he had no male siblings, in which case he fought against his sister. Sometimes he would even take a shot at his cousin. Sooner or later, this resulted in a horrendous amount of devastation, particularly in the South, where things got so bad that Clark Gable, in what is probably the most famous scene from the entire Civil War, turned to Vivien Leigh, and said, ''Frankly, my dear, I don't think we're in Kansas anymore.''

—Dave Barry, *Dave Barry Slept Here*

If the context is appropriate and the allusion is apt, the right reference can establish a quick and easy connection between the author and the reader. If the context is not appropriate, that same allusion will alienate or confuse the reader.

The formal style is not necessarily more complicated than the familiar—but it can be, especially when it uses long words, periodic sentences and subordinate clauses, and other rhetorical devices to excess.

George Orwell provides an example of classic formal style—an excerpt from the King James version of Ecclesiastes—and translated it into twentieth-century jargon to show how simple the formal really was. First, the passage from Ecclesiastes:

I returned, and saw under the sun, that the race is not to the swift, nor the battle to the strong, neither yet bread to the wise, nor yet riches to men of understanding, nor yet favour to men of skill; but time and chance happeneth to them all.

—Ecclesiastes, IX, 11

This is Orwell's translation of the same passage into contemporary jargon:

Objective consideration of contemporary phenomena compels the conclusion that success or failure in competitive activities exhibits no tendency to be commensurate with innate capacity, but that a considerable element of the unpredictable must invariably be taken into account.

—George Orwell, "Politics and the English Language"

There are only two polysyllabic words in the Ecclesiastes quote: *understanding,* which is not abstract or difficult, and *happeneth,* which is only an archaic form of the third-person singular of *to happen.* Despite the formal style of the King James Bible, the effect is simple and direct. Fifteen of the thirty-eight words in Orwell's "translation" have three or more syllables. The effect is convoluted and unclear.

Good writers use the formal and familiar intuitively. The rest of us, who only aspire to good writing, must cultivate the ability to use the formal when a dignified tone is appropriate and the familiar when a conversational tone is wanted.

☞*Try your hand:*
Write a letter to a friend on a social or political issue about which you feel particularly passionate.

Write it in your own words, in familiar style, without regard to rules or techniques. Speak into a tape recorder if necessary, but try to capture the natural rhythm of the way you speak.

Now, using as many formal techniques and figures of speech as you can, write the same letter to your congressperson or to the editor of a magazine or newspaper. Replace the rhythms of speech with the rhythms of tropes. Use repetition and ellipsis and metaphor. Use multisyllabic, Latinate nouns and adjectives.

Then, at some point in the middle, when you are about to touch on the most personal and deeply felt part of your argument, *abandon all formal techniques and return to your natural, familiar style.*

Now rewrite the familiar section using formal techniques. Which way do you like better? Which is more effective?

INFORMAL AND FAMILIAR

Familiar writing is not at all the same thing as *informal speech*. Informal speech is what we use in everyday life when we are speaking freely and casually. *Familiar writing* creates the illusion of informal speech to achieve a direct connection between the writer and the audience.

Writers in search of a personal style must understand the difference between natural informal speech and an effective familiar writing style.

Some of the hallmarks of *informal speech* are:

- Simple vocabulary
- Use of slang and profanity
- Use of less rigorous grammar
- Use of contractions
- Use of simple and incomplete sentences
- Use of irony and humor

What constitutes simple vocabulary varies from speaker to speaker, but most people do not use many polysyllabic words in normal conversation. Most of us use some sort of slang and varying levels of profanity, especially when we use low diction. At times we all use grammar that stretches the rules. We write, "Whom did she marry?" We say, "Who did she marry?" Contractions like "I'm" and "we're" are common; other contracted expressions like "gonna" and "gotta" and "lotta" are less so. Simple sentences make up a good deal of informal speech; loose, disjointed sentences and sentence fragments are common. Finally, irony and humor project a personal attitude toward the subject at hand.

All the elements of informal speech are present in this excerpt from Studs Terkel's *American Dreams: Lost and Found,* one of the author's many oral histories of the United States. The words belong to a seventy-eight-year-old New York City widow named Ruth Curry:

"I would never stick to anything long enough to really make something of myself. I was always busy getting married, a four-time loser. I musta been a little bitch at heart. At seventeen, I married a boy who was like my brother. Hell of a nice boy. I married him to get out of the nest. I got a kick out of guys being crazy about me. I always had guys: New York, Chicago, everywhere.

''There's many guys had more fun with me than goin' to bed with me, 'cause I was a lousy lay. My heart wasn't in it. I was always thinkin' about somethin' else. When I was listenin' to the races, one of my husbands said: 'I'll bet if you were in the throes of an orgasm, you'd say: ''Oh, my god, I gotta get the scratches.'' ' (Laughs.)''

A *familiar writing style* includes the judicious use of these speech characteristics, along with the following additional characteristics that distinguish it from formal style:

• Directness
• Concrete and vivid imagery
• Anglo-Saxon rather than Latinate or polysyllabic language
• A prevalence of short, declarative sentences
• Minimal use of subordinate clauses
• Use of direct address and the first person
• Use of personal reactions and experience
• Use of dialogue

Directness is a characteristic of the familiar, just as indirection is characteristic of the formal. The familiar uses concrete and vivid imagery, often to the exclusion of metaphor and allusion. Vocabulary in the familiar is largely confined to Anglo-Saxon words of one and two syllables; three-syllable adjectives may be used, but longer words and words of Latinate derivation are avoided. Sentence structure is kept simple, with a minimum of subordinate clauses and few periodic sentences. However, interjections, interrupted speech, and loose, digressive sentences reflect normal trains of thought. Direct address makes a personal appeal to the reader, as do first-person accounts and reactions. The goal, in general, is the projection of a personal voice.

The two examples that follow demonstrate uses of the familiar:

Every detail of the pilot-house was familiar to me, with one exception,—a large-mouthed tube under the breast-board. I puzzled over that thing a considerable time; then gave up and asked what it was for.

"To hear the engine-bells through."

It was another good contrivance which ought to have been invented half a century sooner. So I was thinking when the pilot asked,—

"Do you know what this rope is for?"

I managed to get around this question, without committing myself.

"Is this the first time you were ever in a pilot-house?"

I crept under that one.

"Where are you from?"

"New England."

"First time you have ever been West?"

I climbed over this one.

"If you take an interest in such things, I can tell you what all these things are for."

I said I should like it.

                          —Mark Twain, *Life on the Mississippi*
                          (XXIV: "My Incognito Is Exploded")

H. L. Mencken called Mark Twain the "first American author of world rank to write in a genuinely colloquial and native American." Read him today and you still hear a personal voice. The familiar American tone he pioneered inspired a great deal of later familiar prose, from contemporary fiction to the prose of newspaper columnists.

> The detective put two photo albums on my desk and said: "If he's there, you might recognize him."
> The albums were huge. They were filled with front and side pictures of thugs, stick-up men, muggers, pimps, purse snatchers and all-around thieves.
> Halfway through, I said: "You must have every bum in Chicago in here."
> The cop shook his head. "No. Those are just the ones from your area."
> It was an awesome thought: all those mean, moronic mugs plying their trade in my neighborhood alone. And if you add together all the mugs in the other neighborhoods, they're the size of an army. In fact, there are probably many nations whose armies aren't as big as Chicago's street mug population. Or as mean. Or as well armed.
> In a way it made me feel better about having been robbed. If there were that many of them out there, being robbed seemed almost natural. Not being robbed was unnatural.
> —Mike Royko, "I've Fully Paid My Victim Tax"
> (*The Chicago Tribune,* June 28, 1984)

Creating your own style is a matter of understanding your natural informal speaking voice, knowing how to translate that natural voice into a comfortable and familiar writing style, and being able to apply the techniques of formal and familiar style to suit your taste, your purpose, and the tone appropriate for your subject and audience.

One note about tastes: Most writers form their initial preferences in writing style on an appreciation of the good writing of others. Norman Mailer said that his style was formed by Herman Melville: "I'm not saying I write as well as Melville," he said, "but my style was absolutely shaped by his love of long, rolling sentences that contain inversions and reverses and paradoxes and ironies and exclamation points and dashes." And Gore Vidal said, "I was certainly under Hemingway's spell when I was very young, as we all were. I thought his prose was perfect until I read Stephen Crane and realized where he got it all from." And Hemingway himself gave this list of his stylistic influences:

Mark Twain, Flaubert, Stendhal, Bach, Turgenev, Tolstoy, Dostoyevsky, Chekhov, Andrew Marvell, John Donne, Maupassant, the good Kipling, Thoreau, Captain Marryat, Shakespeare, Mozart, Quevedo, Dante, Vergil, Tintoretto, Hieronymous Bosch, Breughel, Patinir, Goya, Giotto, Cézanne, Van Gogh, Gauguin, San Juan de la Cruz, Góngora . . . I put in painters, or started to, because I learn as much from painters about how to write as from writers.

Allow yourself to be inspired by other writers, but try to avoid imitation.

The following exercise will show you how to use the familiar to develop a sense of your own personal style.

☞*Try your hand:*

Speaking into a tape recorder, describe the way something or someone has influenced you, for better or worse. It could be a teacher; an author; a political or spiritual leader; a parent, friend, or loved one; a loss or a separation, such as a divorce or a death; a disease, addiction, or physical infirmity; anything that has profoundly affected the way you live your life.

Speak freely, without worrying about sense or coherence. Free-associate, but concentrate on specific incidents and emotions.

Now transcribe the tape recording. Keep intact all pauses, interruptions, and substandard grammar.

Now edit your informal speech into effective familiar prose: Delete what is incoherent and tie together the unconnected thoughts, but maintain the feeling of a natural voice. If necessary, rewrite to give structure to the thoughts expressed.

Now, decide on a purpose or occasion for the writing exercise and rewrite it, using some of the techniques of formal style; base your choices on your own taste and a sense of appropriateness.

Put the exercise away and pick it up an hour or two later. Listen to the sound of the prose: Does it sound natural? Is it effective? Are you comfortable with this as your voice?

FIVE

Grammar

"Prose is architecture," said Hemingway, "not interior decoration."

The architecture of a good sentence gives it clarity, grace, and power. That architecture is known unglamorously as grammar, the manner in which sentences are constructed. Just as beauty can be found in architectural examples ranging from the simplest house to the grandest cathedral, so can beauty be found in examples of sentences from the plain and simple to the complex and ornate.

One kind of grammatical power can be seen in the construction of a simple declarative sentence or statement, like this opening of Faulkner's short story "That Evening Sun":

- Monday is no different from any other weekday in Jefferson now.

Or this even sparer, mood-setting opening to Eudora Welty's *The Optimist's Daughter:*

- A nurse held the door open for them.

Or this typically hard-boiled one, from James M. Cain's *The Postman Always Rings Twice:*

• They threw me off the hay truck about noon.

What makes these sentences simple, in grammatical terms, is that they have a single clause—a single subject and verb. Grammar aside for the moment, what makes these sentences powerful—perhaps even beautiful—is their ability to say a lot with few words and to imply even more. The beauty of a simple sentence comes from what it does *not* do: It does not complicate or clutter.

A different kind of beauty can be seen in the construction of a more complex sentence, like the opening sentence of Doris Lessing's "My Father":

• We use our parents like recurring dreams, to be entered into when needed; they are always there for love or for hate; but it occurs to me that I was not always there for my father.

This is made up of three sentences, joined by semicolons, with several modifying phrases and a dependent clause, altogether giving it four subjects and four verbs. Grammar again aside for the moment, what makes this sentence special is its insight, the path of its logic, and its surprising conclusion.

Discussions of grammar are almost always tedious: lists of rules; charts of noun declensions and verb conjugations; and countless grammatical terms, each defined and illustrated, overwhelming the curious reader.

To try to avoid those pitfalls, we will start with a few assumptions: one, that you know that a noun is the name of a person, place, thing, or quality; two, that you know a verb represents an action or a state of being; three, that you know the difference between adjectives and adverbs (although you may mix them up sometimes); and four, that you're not absolutely sure, for example, which is correct: "between you and me" or "between you and I" —or, if you are, you're not sure why.

For those who would like one, here is a brief review of the parts of speech, reduced to only those terms essential to a good understanding of how words work:

Nouns

COMMON NOUNS name the class of a person, place, or thing: *farmer, mountain, rock*

PROPER NOUNS name a particular person, place, or thing: *Joe, Paris, New Yorker*

COLLECTIVE NOUNS name a group or unit: *government, committee*

ABSTRACT NOUNS name an idea or quality: *life, love, democracy*

Pronouns

PERSONAL PRONOUNS refer to the speaker: *I/me, you, he/him, she/her, it, we, you, they/them*

RELATIVE PRONOUNS (*who, which, that*) relate a clause back to an antecedent: "The house (antecedent) that (relative pronoun) Jack built is over there."

INTERROGATIVE PRONOUNS ask a question: *who? which? what?*

DEMONSTRATIVE PRONOUNS point out a person or thing: *this, that, these, those*

INDEFINITE PRONOUNS imply but do not refer to a specific antecedent: *any, anyone, each, either, every, everyone, everything, nobody, nothing, one, some, someone*

REFLEXIVE PRONOUNS combine a personal pronoun with *-self* or *-selves: myself, yourself, himself, herself, itself, ourselves, yourselves, themselves*

RECIPROCAL PRONOUNS combine an indefinite pronoun with *other* or *another: each other, one another*

Verbs

TRANSITIVE VERBS have an object, a recipient of the action involved: ''He hit me!''

INTRANSITIVE VERBS do not have an object: ''Sit down!''

LINKING or COPULATIVE VERBS are verbs of being or seeming: ''I am happy,'' ''She looks sad.''

VERBS OF BEING	VERBS OF SEEMING
to appear	to feel
to be	to hear
to become	to look
to grow	to sound
to remain	to smell
to prove	to taste

These verbs take predicate adjectives (see below) and not adverbs.

Adjectives

DESCRIPTIVE ADJECTIVES modify a noun or pronoun: *happy, sad*

LIMITING ADJECTIVES make a noun or pronoun more exact: *one, hers*

PREDICATE ADJECTIVES modify the subject of the linking verbs above: "I feel bad," "She seems sad," "Dinner smells good," "You look pretty."

Adverbs

ADVERBS tell when, where, how, how much, or how often something happened: *yesterday, here, happily, twice*

CONJUNCTIVE ADVERBS connect two independent clauses to form a compound sentence:

accordingly	nevertheless
also	only
besides	so
consequently	still
further	then
hence	therefore
however	too
moreover	

Conjunctions

COORDINATING CONJUNCTIONS connect words, phrases, and clauses of equal rank: *and, but, or, nor*. They are lowercased in titles and headings.

SUBORDINATING CONJUNCTIONS connect a subordinate

clause to an independent clause. They should never be lowercased in titles and headings.

after	that
although	unless
as	when
because	where
if	which
since	while

Prepositions

PREPOSITIONS show the relation of a noun or pronoun to another word:

about	from
above	in
after	of
at	on
before	over
below	to
by	up
for	

Prepositions of four or fewer letters should be lowercased in titles and headings. (See list on pages 205–206.)

Interjections

INTERJECTIONS express sudden, strong emotion: *O!, oh!, hey!, ho!, pish!, tush!, alas!, alack!, yo!*

SENTENCES AND CLAUSES

The architecture of sentences divides them in three primary categories, each of which you use every day: simple, compound, and complex.

A *simple sentence* expresses a thought in one clause—a single unit combining a subject and verb. The subject typically is the actor, the verb is the action or state involved, and the object upon which the action is performed is called the *direct object*. The following are all simple sentences:

- I love.
- I love you.
- Everybody loves a lover.
- Give me your love.

Each of these sentences has a subject and a verb: "I" in the first two, "everybody" in the third, and "you" in the last, although it is merely implied. The technique of isolating subjects and verbs was once taught as a fundamental grammatical skill: "parsing." The art of parsing consisted of reducing any statement, no matter how complex, to its grammatical elements.

In the middle two examples, "you" and "a lover" are the direct objects. In the last example there are two objects: "your love" is the direct object of the verb "give," but the verb here also takes an *indirect object*—an object for whose benefit the action is taken: in this case, "me." An indirect object can often be rephrased with the preposition "to": "Give your love to me."

If it is a command, a sentence can have its subject

implied—as in "Give me your love"—but to be grammatically complete it must always have a verb. A single word can be a sentence if it is a verb in the form of a command: "Sing!"

If a sentence has no verb at all, it is not a sentence; it is a *sentence fragment,* what E. B. White called a "stillborn sentence." These two fragments from typical contemporary advertising copy have no verbs:

• Peace. The grandest wish of all.
• A shade, a smell, a sound, a feeling, a voice in the back of your mind.

Sentence fragments are very often effective uses of language, but they are not sentences. The periods at the end of each are for visual purposes only—to add punch—and serve no grammatical function. Overusing sentence fragments can make your writing seem choppy. Or illiterate. Use them judiciously, and only when effective.

Sentences can be simple but have compound elements. The following sentence from Willa Cather's *My Mortal Enemy* has a *compound subject:*

• He and Myra met as if for the first time, and fell in love with each other.

It also has a *compound verb,* or more precisely, a *compound predicate* (a predicate being the verb and everything—like objects and complements—connected to it):

• He and Myra met as if for the first time, and fell in love with each other.

The second verb, "fell," does not have its own subject. Strictly speaking, the comma is unnecessary with a compound predicate—it is necessary only when there is a new subject—but many writers would say that this comma is necessary for "rhythm." (For more on necessary and unnecessary commas, see Appendix I: The Random House Style Manual.)

The well-written simple sentence requires little effort from the reader to comprehend its message. It is clear and unambiguous. Even when it expresses a complex thought, the simplicity brings clarity. But very little in life can be expressed solely in simple, declarative sentences. That is what *compound* and *complex* sentences are for.

Compound Sentences

Two or more simple statements can be joined together in several ways. The simplest way is to connect them with a word like "and" or "but"—called *coordinating conjunctions,* because they coordinate separate elements. Simple sentences joined by a coordinating conjunction or a semicolon are known as *independent clauses* when they become parts of the same sentence. When two or more of these independent clauses are joined, the result is called a *compound sentence.*

The Cather sentence quoted above could be rewritten as a compound sentence, with two independent clauses, by adding a subject before the second verb:

- He and Myra met as if for the first time, and <u>they</u> fell in love with each other.

A compound sentence is effective when a strong connection between the two points is desired, as it was in the following lead from a *New York Times* article by Nicholas Kristof, written in China shortly before the crackdown in Tiananmen Square:

- BEIJING, May 4 [1989] — A defiant and enthusiastic crowd of more than 100,000 workers and students forced its way through police cordons in the capital today to demand more democracy, and smaller demonstrations were held in many other cities around China.

By using a compound sentence, the author makes the point that the event described is directly related to what is happening in the second part of the sentence — in this case, that defiant and enthusiastic crowds can be found all over the country. Two separate sentences might not make the connection so clearly:

- A defiant and enthusiastic crowd of more than 100,000 workers and students forced its way through police cordons in the capital today to demand more democracy. Smaller demonstrations were held in many other cities around China.

A compound sentence may comprise three or more independent clauses, as it does in the following sentence, from the same reporter, still in China, only five weeks later:

- BEIJING, June 11 — The bloodstains are scarcely visible on the pavement now, the once ubiquitous posters calling for greater freedom are now only tattered shreds, and no one dares protest.

The list here becomes a litany, and the compound sentence is the most effective option. Three separate sentences would dissipate the effect:

- The bloodstains are scarcely visible on the pavement now. The once ubiquitous posters calling for greater freedom are now only tattered shreds. No one dares protest.

A compound sentence is simply two simple sentences joined together by a coordinating conjunction, but a complex sentence is more complex.

Complex Sentences

Sometimes a sentence contains several thoughts, only one of which is of primary importance. Joining them with a coordinating conjunction would not be effective. A clause subordinate to another in logic must be subordinate in grammar as well. In such cases, use a *complex sentence.*

A complex sentence includes one or more independent clauses and at least one *dependent clause.* A dependent clause is a subordinate, explanatory clause that contains a subject and a verb, just like an independent clause, but instead of a coordinating conjunction like ''and'' or ''but'' it begins with a word like ''when,'' ''where,'' ''because,'' ''as,'' "while," "although," "that," or "which." These words are called *subordinating conjunctions,* and they subordinate the *dependent clause* to an independent clause.

The following sentences from Wallace Stegner's *Crossing to Safety* are complex, each with a dependent clause connected to an independent clause by a subordinating conjunction:

• At eleven-thirty, <u>when the locomotive bell on the porch of the Big House clanged</u>, we gathered for swimming, sunning, and conversation on the dock or the elephant rocks.
• I started after her, but <u>as I went through the door</u> I could not keep my eyes from going back to the bed.

These two sentences from Langston Hughes's "Slave on the Block" illustrate the use of two controversial types of dependent clauses — relative clauses that begin with *that* or *which:*

• Perhaps their house in the Village was too far from Harlem, or too hard to find, being back in one of those queer and expensive little side streets <u>that had once been alleys</u> before the art invasion came.
• They hired him to look after the garden, <u>which was just about as big as Michael's grand piano</u> — only a little square behind the house.

The following sentence, the lead of a *New York Times* article by Serge Schmemann, is also a complex sentence with a subordinating conjunction, a dependent clause, and an independent clause:

- WEST BERLIN, Nov. 10 [1989] — <u>As hundreds of thousands of East Berliners romped through the newly porous wall in an unending celebration</u>, West German leaders today proclaimed this the moment Germans had yearned for through forty years of division.

Delete the subordinating conjunction ''as,'' put an ''and'' in the middle, and here is the same sentence — but less effective — as a compound sentence:

- Hundreds of thousands of East Berliners romped through the newly porous wall in an unending celebration, and West German leaders today proclaimed this the moment Germans had yearned for through forty years of division.

   The third option, breaking the complex sentence into two simple sentences, would lose the cause-and-effect quality the writer so clearly desired:

- Hundreds of thousands of East Berliners romped through the newly porous wall in an unending celebration. West German leaders today proclaimed this the moment Germans had yearned for through forty years of division.

   These are the types of choices available to you as you create and edit your writing. A clear understanding of the grammatical possibilities open to you will enable you to choose effectively. Now let's look at some of the problems writers have with different types of clauses.

PROBLEMS WITH CLAUSES

First, two distinctions:

1. The difference between a *clause* and a *phrase* is that a clause has a subject and verb in it; a phrase does not.
2. The difference between an *independent clause* and a *dependent clause* is that an independent clause could exist as a sentence; a dependent clause could not.

Writers have particular problems with a specific kind of dependent clause: the *relative* clause, which is a clause that modifies a noun and usually begins with *who, which,* or *that.* There are two types of relative clauses: *restrictive* and *nonrestrictive.* A third distinction:

3. The difference between a *restrictive* and a *nonrestrictive* clause is that a restrictive clause identifies the word it modifies; a nonrestrictive clause does not. A restrictive clause is essential to the meaning of a sentence; a nonrestrictive clause is not.

The next sentence, from Hemingway's *The Sun Also Rises,* contains two nonrestrictive clauses, both of which could be deleted without losing the essential meaning of the sentence:

• By that time Cohn, <u>who had been regarded purely as an angel</u>, and <u>whose name had appeared on the editorial page merely as a member of the advisory board</u>, had become the sole editor.

Delete the nonrestrictive clauses, and the essential meaning remains:

• By that time Cohn had become the sole editor.

The nonrestrictive clause, encased by commas, does not identify — or restrict — the noun it modifies. It gives additional information about the noun. It is not essential to the meaning of the sentence as a whole. The two nonrestrictive clauses above give us information about Cohn, but they do not identify him.

In the next sentence, also from *The Sun Also Rises,* the "who" clause is restrictive because it restricts the meaning of the word *lady* to a particular woman. It identifies which lady is being written about:

• He had been taken in hand by a lady who hoped to rise with the magazine.

Delete the restrictive clause, and the essential meaning Hemingway had in mind is gone, although the sentence still has a subject and verb and is still a complete grammatical sentence:

• He had been taken in hand by a lady . . .

Here is another restrictive *who* clause, from a 1944 E. B. White *New Yorker* piece called "Summertime":

• Summertime this year is a ripe girl who finds herself forsaken by the boys, the ordinarily attentive and desirous boys.

Writers are especially confused about these clauses when faced with the which/that controversy. In his 1926 *Modern English Usage,* Fowler first made the plea that a standard be set for the difference between these two words. Nonrestrictive clauses, he decreed, should be set off by a comma and the word *which;* restrictive clauses should have no comma and the word *that.*

The rule never really caught on in England, but it became "standard American style" after it was endorsed by Wilson Follett's *Modern American Usage, The Chicago Manual of Style, Words into Type, The New York Times Manual of Style and Usage,* and the *Associated Press Style Manual.* Nevertheless, many American writers, particularly those used to a childhood of British literature, prefer the restrictive *which.*

The following two sentences from Gore Vidal's "The National Security State" illustrate the recommended usage of the restrictive *that* and the nonrestrictive *which.* Note the commas surrounding the nonrestrictive *which* clause and the absence of commas with the restrictive *that* clauses:

- Actually, the real enemy were those National Security Statesmen who had so dexterously hijacked the country, establishing military conscription in peacetime, overthrowing governments that did not please them, and finally keeping all but the very rich docile and jittery by imposing income taxes that theoretically went as high as 90 percent.
- The press, which should know better, is of no help.

In his historical fiction, however, Vidal uses the restrictive *which* to achieve a distinct period sound. The restrictive *which* in this sentence from Vidal's *Empire* should, according to the rule, be a *that* because the clause is restrictive:

• Hearst entered the main hall of the house <u>which</u> he would never, short of an armed revolution, occupy.

Many writers would consider a *that* here awkward:

• Hearst entered the main hall of the house <u>that</u> he would never, short of an armed revolution, occupy.

The *that* could also be deleted entirely. With restrictive clauses, the pronoun is often unnecessary, and the best solution may be no *which* or *that* at all:

• Hearst entered the main hall of the house he would never, short of an armed revolution, occupy.

PROBLEMS WITH PHRASES

First, let's repeat one distinction as a definition: The difference between a *clause* and a *phrase* is that a clause has a subject and verb in it; a phrase does not. A phrase is not just any group of words without a subject-verb combination: It must function as a unit. There are four common types of phrases: *prepositional, infinitive, participial,* and *gerund.* Participial phrases probably cause the most problems for writers.

A prepositional phrase consists of a preposition and its object, like these from Harold Brodkey's short story "On the Waves," the title of which is itself a prepositional phrase:

- <u>In the churning wake</u> of a motorboat <u>from one</u> of the luxury hotels, the gondola bobbed <u>with graceful disequilibrium</u>.

An infinitive phrase consists of an infinitive (*to* followed by a verb) and its object or modifier, as in these examples from the "Overture" to the C. K. Scott-Moncrieff translation of Marcel Proust's *Swann's Way:*

- And half an hour later the thought that it was time <u>to go to sleep</u> would awaken me; I would try <u>to blow out the light</u>; I had been thinking all the time, while I was asleep, of what I had just been reading, but my thoughts had run to a channel of their own, until I myself seemed actually <u>to have become the subject</u> of my book: a church, a quartet, the rivalry between François I and Charles V.

A participial phrase consists of a present or past participle (a verb form that can be used as an adjective: *falling* or *fallen*) and its object or modifiers, like this from Ray Bradbury's "Dandelion Wine":

- <u>Crossing the lawn</u> that morning, Douglas Spaulding broke a spider web with his face.

Participial phrases create problems for writers when they become the notorious *dangling partici-*

ples, participles not attached to the word they modify. This occurs when the participle fails to refer to the subject of the sentence. "Crossing," the participle in the example above, does not dangle because it modifies the subject, Douglas Spaulding, who crossed the lawn that morning. But if Bradbury had written the sentence with the spider web as the subject, the participle would dangle:

• Crossing the lawn that morning, a spider web brushed against Douglas Spaulding's face.

The dangling participle would imply that the spider web crossed the lawn. A classic dangler:

• Sautéed, broiled, baked, or boiled, you'll love our delicious chickens.

No, you won't—not after you've been sautéed, broiled, baked, or boiled. Dangling participles can be fixed by changing the subject of the sentence:

• Sautéed, broiled, baked, or boiled, our delicious chickens will thrill your guests.

From Hemingway's *Green Hills of Africa* comes this spectacular sentence: ninety-five words' worth of participial and infinitive phrases before the sentence even gets to the subject and verb—"we went":

• Now, heavy socks removed, stepping tentatively, trying the pressure of the leather against the toes, the argument past, she wanting not to suffer, but to keep up and please Mr. J.P., me ashamed at having been a four-letter man about boots, at being righteous against pain, at being righteous at all, at ever being righteous, stopping to whisper about it, it all right now, the boots too, without the heavy socks, much better, me hating all righteous bastards now, one absent American friend especially, certainly never to be righteous again, watching Droopy ahead, we went down the long slant of the trail toward the bottom of the canyon where the trees were heavy and tall and the floor of the canyon, that from above had been a narrow gash, opened to a forest-banked stream.

Notice that the dependent relative clause encased in commas breaks Fowler's rule and uses *that* ("that from above had been a narrow gash"). Technically, it should read "which from above," not "that from above." Alternatively, the commas could be deleted and the *that* allowed to remain.

Look again at the Doris Lessing sentence from the beginning of the chapter:

• We use our parents like recurring dreams, to be entered into when needed; they are always there for love or for hate; but it occurs to me that I was not always there for my father.

It begins with an independent clause— "We use our parents like recurrent dreams"—followed by an dependent, infinitive clause— "to be entered into when needed." Two additional independent clauses follow, each separated by a semicolon; the "piling up" of ideas that is produced contributes to the effectiveness of the sentence. The final two independent clauses could be changed into a compound sentence by replacing the final semicolon with an ordinary compound-sentence comma:

- . . . they are always there for love or for hate, but it occurs to me that I was not always there for my father.

Appositives

Words and phrases, like clauses, can be restrictive or nonrestrictive. *Appositives* are nouns or phrases that rephrase or identify a neighboring noun. They can be restrictive or nonrestrictive. As with clauses, commas are used with the nonrestrictive appositives; no commas are used with restrictive ones.

Thus, if you are speaking about Elizabeth Taylor, you might say:

- Her husband Richard Burton was a great actor.

—without a comma. Elizabeth Taylor had several husbands; therefore the appositive (''Richard Burton'') is restrictive. The sentence *needs* it. Delete the restrictive appositive (''Her husband was a great actor''), and you might be calling Mike Todd or Eddie Fisher a great actor.

However, if you are speaking about the wife of the Victorian explorer Sir Richard Burton, the appositive would not be restrictive:

• Her husband, Sir Richard Burton, was a great explorer.

Lady Burton had only one husband. Delete the appositive, and the sentence ("Her husband was a great explorer") retains its essential meaning.

The same goes for the difference between "my sister, Sam" and "my sister Sam": Use the comma if you have only one sister, in which case the appositive is nonrestrictive. More than one sister, and the appositive is restrictive: It identifies which sister is meant.

It also goes for "Dickens's novel *A Tale of Two Cities*"—he wrote more than one novel, so the appositive is restrictive, and no comma is called for. However, the comma *is* appropriate if the choice of novels has already been narrowed down:

• Dickens's great novel of the French Revolution, *A Tale of Two Cities* . . .

PROBLEMS WITH NOUNS AND PRONOUNS

Pronouns and nouns cause problems because they have cases—the subjective case (the form used as the subject of a verb), the possessive case, and, for pronouns, the objective case (the case used for the object of a verb or preposition). Let's look at seven common problems:

PRONOUN PROBLEM 1. A pronoun used as the object of a verb or a preposition must be in the objective case, even when the subjective seems more "refined."

- between you and me (not *I*)
- wait for Mother and me (not *I*)
- They invited Sue and him (not *he*).
- Will you let her and me (not *she* and *I*) sit together?

Don't let the compound object confuse you. Try deleting one of the objects as a test: "wait for *me*," "invited *him*."

Things get a little more complicated with *who* vs. *whom*. In strict grammatical terms, the situation is simple enough: *Whom* is the objective form, *who* the subjective:

- Whom (not *who*) did you wish to see?
- To whom (not *who*) did you give my message?
- Whom (not *who*) should I find there but my cousin?
- I did not know whom (not *who*) to send.

but:

- Who (not *whom*) shall I say is calling?

Use *who* when the person in question is doing the acting and *whom* after a preposition or when the action is being done to the person. In the last example above, *whom* is incorrect because it is the subject of the verb *is calling;* it only seems to be the object of *shall I say,* which is merely parenthetical.

In practice, many people do not follow the rules for *who/whom*. In ordinary conversation, it is probably best to follow your own instincts. If *whom* sounds stilted to you, feel free not to use it:

- INFORMAL: Who did you want to speak to?

In formal writing, though, or writing for publication, it is probably best to keep *who* and *whom* in their proper grammatical places.

PRONOUN PROBLEM 2. A pronoun used as the subject of a clause should be in the subjective case.

• We have no information about who (not *whom*) the other person was.
• Give the money to whoever (not *whomever*) needs it most.

In these examples, *who* and *whoever* appear to be the objects of prepositions, but they are not. The actual objects of these prepositions are the entire clauses that follow them. Within these clauses, *who* and *whoever* are the subjects. This can be seen more easily by getting rid of the rest of the sentence:

• . . . who the other person was.
• . . . whoever needs it most.

A pronoun must be in the case appropriate to the clause it is in.

PRONOUN PROBLEM 3. A noun or pronoun used to modify a gerund—a verb form ending in *-ing* that acts like a noun—should be in the possessive case.

• We are in favor of your (not *you*) bringing the case to a speedy close.

This rule applies even when, as here, the gerund seems to be the object of a preposition.

PRONOUN PROBLEM 4. In formal speech and writing, a pronoun used after the verb "be," or any linking verb, should be in the subjective case.

• This is he (not *him*).
• I would do so if I were she (not *her*).
• It is we (not *us*) who are to blame.

The pronoun after *be* is not a direct object; it is what is known as a *subjective complement*. The linking verb equates the subject with the complement, and the two should be grammatically similar. The complement should be in the same (subjective) case as the subject that precedes it. Think of the verb "be" as an equals sign:

• This is (=) he.
• If I were (=) she . . .

This is an example, however, of a rule that many people choose not to follow. After ringing a doorbell and hearing the question "Who is it?," which would you say: "It's me" or the more technically correct "It is I"?

PRONOUN PROBLEM 5. In formal speech and writing, a pronoun used after *than* or *as* should be in the subjective case.

• They have more friends than I (not *me*).
• I know it as well as they (not *them*).
• She is younger than he (not *him*).

People often assume that the pronoun here is the object of the preposition *than* or *as* and use the objective case. In traditional grammar, it is not. *Than* and *as* are considered conjunctions here, and the pronoun is the subject of the unspoken clause they introduce:

- They have more friends than I (have).
- I know it as well as they (know it).
- She is younger than he (is).

Mentally complete the unspoken clause and the choice of pronoun becomes clear. Remember the rules given earlier: *A pronoun must be in the case appropriate to the clause it is in; a pronoun used as the subject of a clause should be in the subjective case.*

Pronouns also cause problems because they have to agree with the words they replace — their antecedents.

PRONOUN PROBLEM 6. A pronoun must agree with its antecedent in gender, number, and person even when the antecedent seems to be of a different number. Traditional grammar requires this agreement:

- Let everyone attend to his (not *their*) work.
- Everyone in the convent has her (not *their*) own room.

The antecedent (*everyone*) is grammatically singular and takes a singular verb. But singular pronouns like *every, everyone,* and *everybody* have always sounded plural—even to Shakespeare:

- "God send everyone their heart's desire." (*As You Like It*)

Much to the frustration of the rule makers, Shakespeare—along with other writers, such as Swift, Austen, Shelley, Dickens, and Fitzgerald—didn't always follow the rules.

This problem of matching a pronoun to its antecedent has been intensified with the coming of nonsexist language. The third-person plural, being non–gender specific, is often used to avoid the grammatically correct but cumbersome *his or her:*

- Everyone who would like to go should raise their hands.

Fastidious editors and grammarians object to this, pointing out that the verb is singular. Others find the grammatically—but not politically—correct "Everyone who would like to go should raise *his* hand" equally objectionable. Why, they ask with good logic, should the male pronoun be any more universal than the female pronoun? Those who object to this male pronoun may do so on grounds of both sexism and sense: Words like *everyone* seem naturally plural.

Some writers choose to alternate between *his* and *her:*

- Everyone who wishes to go should raise his hand.
- Everyone who wishes to stay should leave hers down.

This, of course, may lead to confusion. Another solution is to rewrite the sentence in the second person or the plural:

• If you would like to go, raise your hand.
• All those who would like to go should raise their hands.

No one solution will please everyone.

PRONOUN PROBLEM 7. Avoid using a pronoun with a missing or ambiguous antecedent. It is easy to use pronouns with missing or ambiguous antecedents. The problem is that the antecedent seems clear enough to the writer when writing. It is only when you are looking over the sentence that the ambiguity presents itself:

• John became a lawyer as his father did before him, and he became very wealthy.

Who became wealthy—John or his father?

• Editors work with writers as they struggle to come up with their ideas, capture them on paper, craft them with rewrites, and, finally, communicate them to readers.

Who comes up with whose ideas? What (or who) gets captured on paper, crafted with rewrites, and communicated to readers? Don't rely on context to make things clear.

The pronouns *it, this, these,* and *they* frequently refer to ambiguous antecedents:

- New studies are being conducted all the time. This will someday provide a solution.
- BETTER: The findings of these studies will someday provide a solution.
- It is often amusing to watch people make mistakes.
- BETTER: Watching people make mistakes is often amusing.
- They do this sort of thing very well in New York.
- BETTER: New Yorkers do this sort of thing very well.

The only solution is vigilance: Check every pronoun you use to see that its antecedent is clear.

PROBLEMS WITH VERBS: NUMBERS, VOICES, AND MOODS

Verbs cause even more problems than pronouns because of the far greater number of forms they can take. Without stopping to conjugate verbs in all their forms, let's look at the principal problems writers have with them.

Numbers

A verb must agree with its subject in number:

- The majority was (not *were*) overruled.
- The government was (not *were*) disbanded.

In American usage, if the subject refers to the group as a whole it is singular; if it refers to the individual members it is plural: "The audience rose to their (not *its*) feet." This is not so in England: Where we would say "The Bush administration *is* united," they would say "Her Majesty's Government *are* agreed."

Latin-derived plurals are often problematic.

• The data are (or *is*?) correct.

For some nouns there is a clear preference: *criteria, phenomena, curricula,* and *strata* are the plural forms of *criterion, phenomenon, curriculum,* and *stratum;* using any of these plural nouns with a singular verb will be widely regarded as an error. On the other hand, there are nouns equally plural in form in their native Latin (or Greek) that now lead quiet lives as English singular nouns; using *agenda, insignia,* and *trivia* as singulars will not raise any eyebrows. Why? The answer is a shaky one at best: because we don't generally use *agendum, insigne,* or *trivium* as English words. Other nouns remain on the singular-plural borderline. It is safer to use these with plural verbs:

• The data are (not *is*) correct.
• The media were (not *was*) permitted in the courtroom.
• Graffiti cover (not *covers*) the walls.

When a verb relates to two or more nouns connected by a coordinate conjunction:

1. If it agrees with them conjointly, it takes the plural:

- The boy and his dog *were* reunited.
- Both the pilot and the copilot were at the controls.

2. If it agrees with them separately it takes the same number as the noun that stands next to it:

- Neither the pilot nor the passengers *were* saved.
- Neither the passengers nor the pilot *was* saved.

3. If it agrees with one and not the other it takes the number of the one in the affirmative:

- The parents and not the child *are* responsible.
- The child and not the parents *is* responsible.

Several pronoun-verb constructions give writers pause:

- She is the only one who understands.
- They are the only ones who understand.

This is true even in the construction "one of those who . . ."—in which the subject is not the singular "one":

- She is one of those <u>people who understand</u> (not *understands*).
- It's just one of those <u>songs that start</u> (not *starts*) going again.

Pronouns like *anybody, anyone, each, either, everybody, everyone, neither, nobody, no one, somebody,* and *someone* take singular verbs:

- Each of us is (not *are*) invited.
- Neither of them is (not *are*) going to be there.

Any and *none* take singular or plural verbs, depending on sense:

- None of us is invited.
- None of the guests are here yet.

When singular and plural subjects are joined by constructions like *both . . . and, either . . . or,* or *not only . . . but,* the verb takes on the number of the subject closest to it:

- Neither the pilot nor the <u>passengers were aware</u> of the disturbance.
- Neither the passengers nor the <u>pilot was aware</u> of the disturbance.

A clause or phrase that comes between the subject and the verb should not affect the number of the verb:

- The initial investment, not to mention the enormous profits, was substantial.

Plural nouns that are singular in meaning take singular verbs:

- Politics makes (not *make*) strange bedfellows.
- Sports has (not *have*) always been her passion.

But:

- Her favorite sports are badminton and field hockey.
- His pajamas were (not *was*) on backward.

Voices

The active voice focuses attention on the doer, the passive voice on what has been done. Sometimes you may want to emphasize what has been done, using the passive voice—especially when you don't know or don't want to say who the doer was (for example, when the doer is unimportant or a vague "they"). But most often, your writing will be more forceful and more concise if you stick to the active voice.

The passive can be recognized by its use of a form of the verb *to be* plus a past participle. (That sentence was in the passive voice.) The following are passive constructions:

- The passive voice is recognized . . .
- The passive voice was recognized . . .
- The passive voice has been recognized . . .
- The passive voice may be recognized . . .
- The passive voice will be recognized . . .

Putting that paragraph opening in the active voice would yield:

- ACTIVE: One can recognize the passive voice by its use of . . .

These passive constructions are fairly recent. The passive voice, as we know it, did not exist in Old English. Even in Shakespeare one finds very little of it.

"The barn is a-building," a more active construction, was used until the eighteenth century, when "The barn is being built" became the common usage it is today.

The passive voice is most stultifying in impersonal constructions like the following:

• It is believed that . . .
• It is to be understood that . . .

Examine all sentences that involve states of being for unnecessary passives:

• There are people who live here who believe . . .

Delete the "There are" and qualify the "people" so the statement is not absolute:

• Many residents believe . . .

Avoiding these forms will give you the elbow room to use a few deliberate passive constructions for a desired effect without unduly weighing down your prose.

Moods

Verbs, like people, have various moods. Two of them—the indicative, used in most statements and questions, and the imperative, used in commands— are fairly straightforward; one—the subjunctive— creates difficulties.

The subjunctive is used incorrectly in one of two

ways: It is either used when it should not be or not used when it should be.

First, when it should be: Use the subjunctive when expressing a conditional statement that is dubious, doubtful, or contrary to known facts:

- "If I Were [not *Was*] King of the Forest" (which I clearly am not)
- "If Love Were [not *Was*] All" (which it, sadly, is not)
- "If I were [not *was*] a carpenter and you were a lady" (which we neither of us are)

The subjunctive is correct in these songs because the conditional statements are contrary to known facts.

Next, when the subjunctive should *not* be used: Not every "if" clause should have a subjunctive. Do not use a subjunctive when the "if" clause introduces an indirect question rather than a conditional statement:

- The waiter asked if I was (not *were*) finished.

In conditional sentences, the subjunctive should not be used when the conditional statement is true or likely:

- If he was (not *were*) guilty, it was because of his upbringing.
- If food was (not *were*) scarce, shelter was nonexistent.
- If I was (not *were*) there, I must have seen her.

But:

- If I were (not *was*) there, I would speak to her myself.

In conditional statements, the subjunctive is often somewhat subjective; you must judge the probability of your propositions and choose the verb form accordingly.

Which is correct:
If it were or if it was?
Use *if it were* when it wasn't and *if it was* when it was.

Some other uses of the subjunctive cause fewer problems. The present subjunctive survives in "that" clauses expressing what is advisable, desirable, suggested, or demanded:

- We insisted that she stay (not *stays*).
- The doctor recommended that he take (not *takes*) some time off.
- It is important that she understand (not *understands*) the reason.

Another, for the most part archaic, use of the subjunctive survives in some set phrases:

- Suffice it to say . . .
- If need be . . .
- Far be it from me . . .
- Lest we forget . . .

- Come what may . . .
- Heaven help us.

These phrases exist today as relics of a once-common form, the present subjunctive.

- Though this be madness, yet there is method in't.
                              —William Shakespeare, *Hamlet*

The subjunctive is often hard to detect: In the past tense, it is only distinguishable with the verb be ("if I *were*"); in the present it is only distinguishable in the third person ("lest he *forget*"). But though it may escape our notice, the mood continues to exist as a useful grammatical feature of the language, one well worth learning, using, and preserving.

Though this be grammar, yet there is method in't.

SIX

Usage

Usage is an ever-changing standard for what people accept as the right way to speak and write. There are different correct standards of usage for speech, for general writing, and for formal writing. These standards change from generation to generation, although those used for writing for publication change more slowly than do the standards of speech. It is easy to confuse the different rules and not know which form of a word or expression is considered acceptable. Indeed, the very nature of usage dictates that previously unacceptable forms become acceptable with time and use.

Nevertheless, it is supposed that the reader of this book wants to know which form will make for better writing. This chapter will describe eighty usages that are important for writers to know, clarifying what is conventionally accepted as ''right'' and ''wrong'' and what is ''acceptable'' and ''unacceptable.'' The choice is always the writer's, but you must understand the distinctions in order to make educated choices.

The entries are arranged in this chapter in groups. The groups and their entries are listed below. The entries are also listed alphabetically in the General Index on page 257.

Three You **Must** Know

shall : will
that : which
who : whom

flaunt : flout
immigrate : emigrate
precede : proceed
stationary : stationery

Ten Mistakes Never to Make

affect : effect
bad : badly
fewer : less
farther : further
hopefully
important : importantly
it's : its
like : as
literally
principal : principle

Seven Problematic
Prepositional Phrases

different from : different
    than
due to : owing to : because
    of
half : half of / off : off of
of : of a
on behalf of : in behalf of
on the street : in the
    street / on line : in line
on to : onto / in to : into

Fifteen Difficult Distinctions

allude : elude
allusion : elusion : illusion :
    delusion
among : between
assume : presume
assure : ensure : insure
bring : take
capital : capitol
compliment : complement
convince : persuade
discreet : discrete
disinterested : uninterested

Fifteen Points Nitpickers
Pick On

any, every
awhile : a while
bimonthly : semimonthly
blonde : blond
depreciate : deprecate
flounder : founder
forgo : forego
get : got : gotten
glimpse : glance

imply : infer
nauseous : nauseated
purposely : purposefully
shrink, shrank, shrunk
whether : whether or not
wrack : rack : wreck : wreak

Thirty-one Words Word Watchers Watch

burglary : robbery
callous : callus
canvas : canvass
casket : coffin
catsup : ketchup
childish : childlike
continually : continuously
cynic : skeptic
defective : deficient
forward : foreword
gourmet : gourmand : glutton
graduated : graduated from : was graduated from
gratified : grateful
hang : hung
lend : loan
lighted : lit
luxuriant : luxurious
oral : aural : verbal
pair of : pairs of

partially : partly
percent : percentage
pitiful : pitiable : piteous
prescribe : proscribe : prescription
prophecy : prophesy
ravish : ravage
sensuous : sensual
spoonsful : spoonfuls
stanch : staunch
try and : try to
whiskey : whisky
Xerox : photocopy

Two Slippery Suffixes

-able : -ible
-ic : -ical

Two Unwitting Briticisms

a : an
-ward : -wards

Five Nonwords

alright
double entendre
momento
preventative
'till

THREE YOU *MUST* KNOW

who : whom
shall : will
that : which

These three have been joined together because people are so often uncertain of their proper use. Nearly everyone stumbles over *who* and *whom;* the differences between *that* and *which* are a mystery to many, and *shall* and *will* can confound even the best writers.

But every writer knows the distinctions exist. Master these three and you will remove a disproportionate amount of doubt from your use of language.

who : whom

Whom is the form of the pronoun used as the direct object of a verb (''Whom did you see?'') and the object of a preposition (''To whom did you speak?'').

It is not correct to use *whom* when it is the subject of a clause that serves as the object of a preposition. ''Give the money to whoever needs it most'' is correct; ''. . . *whomever* needs it most'' is not, because *whoever* is the subject of *needs*.

Sometime after World War II the rule makers decided that *whom* was doomed. ''Who are you speaking to?'' was now acceptable. But people were used to *whom*. It sounded right, and ''To who are you speaking?'' sounded wrong. So, like Mark Twain's death, whom's doom was prematurely proclaimed.

By the way, putting the preposition at the end of a sentence like ''Who are you speaking to?'' has been acceptable for many years. The rule that you should never end a sentence with a preposition was derived from the fact that it is impossible to do so in Latin. Winston Churchill described the extension of this rule into English as the "sort of nonsense up with which I will not put."

You might want to avoid the objective-case *whom* in vernacular expressions like "Who's kidding who?" "Who's kidding whom" would sound over-formal in many situations.

Which is correct?
Who or whom?
Use *whom* after a preposition and when the action is being done to the person in question, but avoid it when it is really the subject of another clause. A simple mnemonic is: Use *whom* if you would use *them* and *who* if you would use *they*.

---

that : which
• This is the rule *that* people break most often.
• This is the rule *which* people break most often.

Which should you use: *which* or *that*?

When writing for publication, *that* is the preferred form with a restrictive clause. The clause "that people break most often" is restrictive — it identifies the word *rule* in a way essential to the meaning of the sentence. *Which* would be correct with a nonrestrictive clause — one that adds information but is not essential to the sentence:

- These are the currently accepted rules, *which* people often break.

Restrictive and nonrestrictive clauses are discussed more fully in the preceding chapter.

Most people break this rule because they think that *which* sounds more literary, more elegant, or more correct. Also, the rule is one of those imposed after centuries of established usage.

The British tend to be indifferent to the distinction. To Americans raised on Dickens and Brontë sister novels, *that* has always sounded inelegant. Why then, you might ask, should the distinction be made at all?

The reason given by the *which* hunters is that if everyone were to use *which* for nonrestrictive phrases and *that* for restrictive ones, we would all be able to rest assured that a *that* clause is restrictive and a *which* clause nonrestrictive. No *which* lover can deny the crisp, restrictive effect Shakespeare achieved with:

- Uneasy lies the head *that* wears the crown.

"Uneasy lies the head *which* wears the crown" lacks punch. Note, however, this lack of consistency in one well-known quote from the King James Bible:

- Render therefore unto Caesar the things *which* are Caesar's; and unto God the things *that* are God's.

Like many issues of usage, this one is a matter of taste. Develop a taste of your own, and let your educated instincts guide you. Remember the house "*that* Jack built," not "*which* Jack built."

Many writers use the comma as their guide. If a comma seems appropriate before the clause, the clause is probably nonrestrictive: Use *which.* If a comma seems intrusive, the clause is probably restrictive: Use *that.*

Which is correct?
Which or that?
Try this simple rule: If you can use *that,* do.

---

shall : will

Once upon a time the rule was simple: To express the simple future, use *shall* in the first person ("I shall go," "We shall go") and *will* in the second and third persons ("You will go," "He/She/One/It/They will go"). To express purpose, determination, obligation, or compulsion, reverse the rule ("I will go," "You shall go").

Shall, it was explained, came from the Old English word *sceal,* which meant "ought" and therefore implied obligation. *Will,* on the other hand, came from the Old English word *wyllan,* which implied intent and determination.

This made a certain amount of sense, and it still does. The problem is that few Americans observe the distinction.

In 1945, for example, General Douglas MacArthur uttered the purposeful and determined "I shall return." According to the rule, he should have said, "I will return." But he didn't. *Shall* just sounded better.

In America, *will* is currently used for the simple future of the first person as well as for that of the second and third. *Shall* may be used with any person to express purpose, determination, obligation, or compulsion—or merely to sound more formal.

Shall continues to linger in a few useful phrases that cloud the issue: ''Shall we dance?'' ''Shall we go?'' ''Shall I?'' The nearest equivalent of this usage would be ''Would you like to . . . ?'' or ''Would you care to . . . ?'' *Will* instead of *shall* here would not mean the same thing at all.

Which is correct?
Shall or will?
Use *shall* for consulting someone else's opinion, preference, wish, or decision: ''Shall we go?'' ''Shall I leave?'' Use *shall,* if you wish, to express your own, first-person purpose, determination, obligation, or compulsion. It is perfectly acceptable, though, to use *will* in all other circumstances.

TEN MISTAKES NEVER TO MAKE

Don't be caught making any of these ten mistakes. You probably know them already, but in case you forgot:

affect : effect
bad : badly
fewer : less

farther : further
hopefully
importantly : important
it's : its
like : as
literally
principal : principle

affect : effect

Affect is used as a noun only rarely, accented on the first syllable, in the psychological sense of "emotional response" ("without visible affect"), so there is no cause to confuse it with the much more common noun *effect* ("producing the desired effect").

There are two different verbs spelled *affect,* however, both pronounced with the stress on the second syllable. One means "to pretend or assume," as in "He affected a blasé, self-assured attitude." The other meaning is "to have an effect on," as in "Her words affected the crowd deeply." This is where the trouble starts.

Effect as a verb means roughly "to bring about" or "to accomplish" ("to effect change"). The confusion comes from the two verbs' similar pronunciation.

bad : badly

If you are ill, you should say, "I feel *bad*" not "I feel *badly,*" just as you would say, "I feel unhappy" not "I feel unhappily."

To feel is one of those linking verbs that take a predicate adjective, not an adverb. (For more on linking verbs see the previous chapter.) People use *badly* because they think an adverb is called for.

It is, however, correct to say, "I don't feel *well*" —because *well* in this case is not the adverb, it is the adjective *well,* the antonym of *unwell.*

Only if you have lost the sense of touch do you feel badly.

fewer : less

"Fewer calories, less fat and cholesterol." This simple rule will serve in most cases: Use *fewer* to modify plural nouns specifying countable units ("fewer projects," "fewer problems"); use *less* to modify singular mass nouns and singular abstract nouns ("less sugar," "less energy").

There are occasions, however, when *less* is used where *fewer* might have been expected, generally in instances when the items are enumerated or are distances, units of time, or sums of money: "less than ten words," "less than fifteen miles from here, "less than ten minutes from now," "less than five dollars." If it's bits and pieces, use *fewer;* if it's the size of a totality, use *less.*

Which is correct?
Fewer or less?
Use *fewer* when counting and *less* when measuring.

---

farther : further
Farther is used for physical, literal, or longitudinal distance, *further* for degree or quantity, or for spatial, temporal, metaphorical, or metaphysical distance. So, "Mars is farther from Venus than Saturn is," but "Nothing could be further from the truth."

"How much farther do we have to go?" but "How much further is it?"

Common usage, however, has made the two words almost

interchangeable. Question: "Is he further (or *farther*?) along than I am?" Answer: "further." To be safe, reserve *farther* for literal distances.

hopefully

When you modify a sentence with this adverb at the beginning, as in "Hopefully, I will win the lottery," you are embracing one of the great usage controversies of modern times and leaving yourself open to vociferous criticism. Although most people will understand that you mean "It is hoped" or "I hope," many will insist that *hopefully* can only mean "in a hopeful manner." Much of the furor comes from the overuse of the word in speech.

If you are writing for publication, you might want to avoid *hopefully* in the controversial sense, although — interestingly enough — other sentence modifiers such as *basically, remarkably, fortunately,* and *interestingly* can be used without fear of such criticism. (See **literally,** page 150.)

importantly : important

More importantly, like *hopefully,* is an adverb without a verb to modify, and also like *hopefully* it is often used as a sentence modifier. When stringing together points, many people use "more importantly" as a connective meaning "it is more important that." Because *is* is a linking verb that takes a predicate adjective and not an adverb, many writers and editors prefer *more important* to *more importantly.*

its : it's

It's surprising how many people confuse these two little words. The apostrophe here, perhaps illogically, has nothing to do with possession, despite the fact that apostrophes routinely denote the possessive case in nouns. This apostrophe is for purposes of contraction only: *it's* is short for *it is*.

The same mistake is sometimes made with *her's* for *hers* and *their's* for *theirs* and less frequently with *our's* for *ours* or *your's* for *yours*. It is also made with *who's* for *whose*.

In all these instances, the apostrophe is used for the apostrophic contraction only. With pronouns, if contraction is intended, use *it's* or *who's;* if possession is involved, use *its* or *whose*.

like : as

There is no problem with *like* in its role as a preposition, before a noun or pronoun: "runs *like* a dream," "that's just *like* her." But you will run into trouble if you use it as a conjunction, instead of *as,* before a subordinate clause with a verb in it: "He's just interested, *like* we all are."

Back when advertisers were inclined to say that cigarettes tasted "good," Winston was touted as tasting "good like a cigarette should," whereas, according to the strictest rules, it should have tasted good *as* a cigarette should. Once people become accustomed to something like this, it becomes colloquial, and the traditional usage seems fussy. (See **shrink, shrank, shrunk,** page 163.)

Many people now routinely use *like* as a conjunction, but you can save yourself criticism by avoiding the conjunctional *like* in your writing.

literally

You can safely use this adverb to mean "in a literal sense," as in "There were literally thousands of locusts." It's the exaggerated meaning of "virtually" that invites an accusation of sloppy writing: "I am *literally* at my wit's end" or, even worse, "I was literally beside myself." The inadvertent hyperbole can lead to outright silliness: "This book will *literally* make you die of laughter."

principle : principal

Even people who can spell well are confused by these two words. Mnemonics abound, but even the best mnemonic is usually helpful only to the inventor. Remember: Only *principal* can be an adjective, meaning "main" or "most important."

Of the two nouns, *principal* is either a person or an amount of money, whereas *principle* refers to a law or a rule.

FIFTEEN DIFFICULT DISTINCTIONS

If you consider yourself a careful writer, you are probably familiar with many if not all of these distinctions. Glance at the list and see how many of them you know:

allude : elude

allusion : elusion : illusion : delusion

among : between

assume : presume

assure : ensure : insure

bring : take

capital : capitol

compliment : complement

convince : persuade

discreet : discrete

disinterested : uninterested

flaunt : flout

immigrate : emigrate

precede : proceed
stationary : stationery

allude : elude

You *allude* to something by referring to it obliquely, but you *elude* your pursuers.

allusion : elusion : illusion : delusion

An *allusion* is a casual reference to something, an *elusion* is an escape or evasion, an *illusion* is a false conception or vision, and a *delusion* is the belief in that false conception or vision.

among : between

The traditional usage rule holds that *between* is used to express a relationship when only two objects are involved (''between the devil and the deep blue sea'') and *among* is used for three or more (''Let's keep this secret among the four of us'').

Between, however, is commonly used to express a relationship of persons or things considered individually, whatever the number, as in ''Between holding down a job, doing the housework, and watching the children, he has very little time for himself.''

Amongst is a variant form of *among* more common in British than in American usage.

assume : presume

To assume is to take something for granted as being true; *to presume* is to suppose with confidence. Thus, Stanley *presumed* to have found Dr. Livingstone; he did not *assume* he had. The man he encountered in the jungle could very well have turned out to be some other doctor.

Each of these words has other meanings: *presume* also means "to act without authority," and *assume* means "to take upon oneself." You presume if you assume someone else's identity.

assure : ensure : insure

You *assure* your mother you will eat well (and *reassure* her if she doubts you). But you eat well to *ensure*—not *insure*—that you stay healthy.

The distinction goes back to H. W. Fowler's 1926 *Dictionary of Modern English Usage.* Fowler said that you *insure* your belongings by buying *insurance,* but you *ensure* when you make sure of something. This can be a useful distinction, but it is made more often in British English than in American English. The editors of *The New York Times* do not make it at all; they use *insure* for "make sure."

If you wish to keep the distinction alive, use *insure* only when dealing with money matters and *ensure* in all other cases.

bring : take

You *bring* something to someone and *take* something from someone. *Take* involves movement away from the speaker or the spoken-of, *bring* involves movement to the speaker or the spoken-of.

For example: "take it away," "take it or leave it," "take me out to the ball game," and "bring home the bacon."

capital : capitol

A *capitol* is a building found in a city called a *capital.*

There are *capital* letters and *capital* ideas, and you put *capital* into an investment, but *capitol* is used only for the building or buildings where the functions of government are carried out.

compliment : complement

To compliment means to praise. With an *e* not an *i*, *to complement* means "to add to": That much-appreciated *compliment* will *complement* the other you gave me yesterday.

convince : persuade

Although these are commonly used as synonyms, there persists a rule that *convince* must be followed by *that* or *of* but not by a verb. *Persuade,* according to this rule, is followed by a verb. Thus, you can *convince* someone *of* something, you can *convince* someone *that* something is so, but you must *persuade* him or her *to do* something.

The rule is to be followed or not, according to your preference.

discreet : discrete

Discreet means "cautious" or "discerning"; *discrete* means "separate" or "distinct." Be discreet, and use them discretely.

disinterested : uninterested

Disinterested implies impartiality, *uninterested* boredom. It's better to plead your case before a *disinterested* tribunal than before an *uninterested* one.

flaunt : flout

This is one instance where advertising helped: "When you've got it, flaunt it": a mnemonic that *to flaunt* means "to show off." When you *flout* something, you disregard it scornfully. Don't flout this distinction; flaunt your knowledge of it.

immigrate : emigrate

At what point does an emigrant ("one who leaves a country") become an immigrant ("one who enters a country")? You *emigrate from* a country, and you *immigrate into* one.

precede : proceed

To precede is to go before, *to proceed* to go forward. It's the spelling that confuses people, and the single *e* in *procedure* further confuses them.

stationary : stationery

Remembering how to keep the spellings of these two words apart can be irksome. Of the two, you will probably need to spell *stationary,* meaning "not moving," far more often than *stationery,* meaning "writing paper."

Mnemonic 1: *Stationery* has the *e*—as in *pen*—or the *er*—as in *paper.*

Mnemonic 2: If you stand still, you're stationary.

SEVEN PROBLEMATIC PREPOSITIONAL PHRASES

Writers are often confused as to which prepositions to use. The seven that follow cause particular problems:

different from : different than
due to : owing to : because of
half : half of / off : off of
of : of a

on behalf of : in behalf of
on the street : in the street / on line : in line
on to : onto / in to : into

different from : different than

Different from ("our house is different from yours") is the prevalent form in American and British usage. *Different than* is considered standard when it is followed by a clause with a verb in it ("The countryside is different than we expected it to be"). The British think of things as *different to* other things.

In the interest of better prose, be sure that what precedes the *different* and what follows it have parallel structures: "The customs of the North are different from the South" should be "The customs of the North are different from *those of* the South."

due to : owing to : because of

For years, schoolteachers and copy editors dutifully changed every *due to* to *owing to*. *Due to* was considered ungrammatical because *due* was an adjective and not a preposition. *Owing* is a present participle, so it should have been just as incorrect, but *owing to* had been in the language longer. *Because of* has always been a grammatically correct alternative: "She left the room *because of* him."

All three prepositional phrases are now considered equally correct.

half : half of / off: off of

Half takes *of* only when modifying a pronoun ("*half of* them were still alive") and never when modifying a noun ("*half* the apples were rotten to the core"). Never, however, use *of* with *off:* "Get *off* my back," not "Get *off of* me."

Half hour and *half an hour* are equally correct. The choice is yours.

of : of a

As the song says, "What *kind of* fool am I?" not "What kind *of a* fool am I?" Similarly, "I'm not that big a fool," not "I'm not that big *of a* fool."

Like *half of* and *off of,* this is one of those little substandard expressions that can make you sound careless.

The rule is: After an adjective, use the indefinite article (*a, an*) without the preposition *of.* After an expression of category (*kind, sort, type*) use the preposition without the article.

on behalf of : in behalf of

A distinction to cherish: *On behalf of* means "in place of"; *in behalf of* means "in the interest of." Therefore, "On behalf of the other members of the committee I would like to present you with this check, which represents the money we raised in behalf of the homeless."

on the street : in the street / on line : in line

The first is a difference in usage between England and the United States, the second between New York City and the rest of the English-speaking world.

In England one lives *in* Downing Street; in America you live *on* Main Street. This was also proper American usage as recently as the turn of the century. The 1900 "Don't List" of the *New York Herald* admonished its reporters: "Don't use 'on' for 'in' a street. The Metropolitan Opera House is 'in' Broadway, not 'on' Broadway."

As for why people wait *on* lines only in New York while everywhere else in the English-speaking world they wait *in* lines, there is no explanation. In England they wait "in line," but more often they wait "*on* a queue," *queue* being French for "tail" or "line."

on to : onto / in to : into

Many writers say *onto* when they mean *on* or *on to*.

Onto means "to a position on." It implies movement from one place to another: "They moved the lectern *onto* the dais."

On to is made up of an adverb—*on* in this case is an adverb—followed by a preposition—*to*. "Let's move *on to* the next topic" or "The clever detective was *on to* something." The adverb modifies the verb that precedes it and becomes part of the verb: *to move on*. Let's move on to *into:*

Again, when movement from one place to another is involved *into* is closed up: "moving *into* a new apartment." The adverb-preposition combination is two words: "going *in to* dinner."

FIFTEEN POINTS NITPICKERS PICK ON

None of the following represents a serious writing gaffe, but anyone truly interested in words and their finer shadings should know these. In many cases, the choice is yours: There is no right and wrong, or the distinction is no longer widely observed.

any, every
awhile : a while
bimonthly : semimonthly
blonde : blond
depreciate : deprecate
flounder : founder

forgo : forego
get : got : gotten
glimpse : glance
nauseous : nauseated
purposely : purposefully
shrink, shrank, shrunk
whether : whether or not
wrack : rack : wreck : wreak

any, every

Anymore and *any more* are acceptable spelling forms for the adverb, but *anymore* is the more common: *Alice Doesn't Live Here Anymore.*

Any more is preferred when *more* is a pronoun or adjective, modified by *any:* ''I don't want any more'' or ''Are there any more doughnuts?'' *Anymore* is commonly used for ''any longer'' or ''nowadays.''

A rule of thumb: Spell the compound as two words when you mean ''any *single* thing'': ''Anyone who wants to come can come, but any one of us can stay home.'' Spell the adverbial forms as one word (*anywhere, anytime,*) unless they are preceded by a preposition (*at any time, in any way*).

With *every-* compounds the rules are similar but different: The pronouns *everybody* and *everyone* are spelled as one word, as is the adjective *everyday* (''an *everyday* event''). But the adverbial phrases *every day, every way,* and—especially—*every time* should be spelled open (''Every Day I Have the Blues,'' ''Ev'ry Time We Say Goodbye'').

awhile : a while

An easy one to get confused about, this distinction depends on the presence or absence of the preposition *for:* You wait *awhile,* or you wait *for a while. Awhile* itself is an adverb that describes how you wait, like *forever* or *patiently*. *While* is a noun — you wait for "a while" just as you might wait for "a minute," "an hour" or "a tardy companion."

bimonthly : semimonthly

Words like *bimonthly* and *semimonthly* are so often used to mean the same thing that it is often impossible to be sure what the user means unless some contextual clue is given: "We will meet semimonthly, on the fourteenth and the twenty-eighth" or "a bimonthly publication appearing six times a year."

Writers seeking to know which is which are advised to use alternate expressions: *every other week* or *twice a month*. For those who persist in knowing absolutely, the following definition is offered, with the caveat that few people may know what you mean: *Semi-* means "twice a" and *bi-* means "every two." No wonder the British use *fortnightly*.

blonde : blond

In French a man with blond hair is a *blond* while a woman is a *blonde*. Many writers and editors feel that the same distinction should be made in English and the adjective should always be spelled without the *e:* "He is a blond; she is a blonde; they both have blond hair."

Others feel that to make this distinction is sexist and that all forms of the word should be spelled *blond* or *blonde*. Again, the choice is yours.

depreciate : deprecate

To depreciate, in the sense of "to lower in value or estimation," has come to be largely associated with monetary matters: "factors that *depreciated* the property." In the sense of "disparage" or "belittle," *depreciate* has to a great extent been replaced by *deprecate*—which formerly meant "express disapproval of" or "protest against," a meaning which is all but gone today. As a result, the derived word *self-depreciating* has almost entirely been replaced by the more common *self-deprecating*.

A few related words: *To denigrate* something is to defame it, *to derogate* from it is to detract from it, and *to depreciate* it is to diminish it, belittle it, or disparage it.

Therefore, when one belittles oneself, one can be, more accurately, *self-denigrating* (self-defaming), *self-derogating* (self-detracting), or *self-depreciating* (self-devaluing), as well as the less precise *self-deprecating*.

flounder : founder

The fish (*flounder*) is a handy mnemonic here: *To flounder* is "to thrash about," as a flounder would do out of water. But if you waited until it was dead and then threw it back into the water, the flounder would founder—it would sink.

forgo : forego

There is a somewhat uncommon verb, *forego*, which means "to go before" or "to precede": "Wherever he travels, his reputation *foregoes* him." *Forego*—with an *e* in the middle—is the only spelling for this verb.

The more common verb *forgo*, which means "abstain or refrain from," is spelled without the *e*: "We've decided to *forgo* further work on the project."

To confuse matters, so many people now spell *forgo* with the incorrect *e* that dictionaries list *forego* as a variant spelling of the word meaning "abstain or refrain from."

Recommendation: Forgo *forego* unless you go before.

get : got : gotten

This is an odd one, because the verb *to get* can mean so many things. The past participle is *got,* not *gotten,* but in spoken American English, *gotten* is a common alternative. It is used in the sense of "received" or "acquired" ("I've *gotten* replies from half the list") more than it is in the sense indicating necessity ("I've *got* to get out of here"). In written English in both cases, *got* is the preferred alternative.

The verb *to get* has always exercised an odd hold over the language, claiming many more meanings than the simple "to acquire." In Eric Partridge's sadly out-of-print *Usage and Abusage,* he quotes an anonymous eighteenth-century satirist, who put all the abuses of the word *get* together:

> When I *got* to Canterbury, I *got* a chaise for town. But I *got* wet through before I *got* to Canterbury, and I *got* such a cold as I shall not be able to *get* rid of in a hurry. . . . As soon as I *got* back to my inn, I *got* my supper, and *got* to bed, it was not long before I *got* to sleep. When I *got* up in the morning, I *got* my breakfast, and then *got* myself drest, that I might *get* out in time. . . . I have *got* nothing particular for you, and so adieu.

glimpse : glance

A *glimpse* is a quick sight of something; a *glance* is a quick look at something. You "catch a glimpse," but you "take a glance." You never "catch a glance" unless one is thrown at you.

imply : infer

This one involves a successful forward pass: I *imply* something by tossing you a few hints. You *infer* my meaning from my hints, and we both nod knowingly.

nauseous : nauseated

This distinction, much argued over, is that *nauseous* used to mean "causing nausea," whereas it has come to mean "affected by nausea."

Thus, "The smell of brussels sprouts nauseates me" was the correct usage, as was "I am nauseated by brussels sprouts," as was "Brussels sprouts are nauseous to me."

The one version that most people use today—"Brussels sprouts make me nauseous"—was formerly incorrect. The choice, again, is yours.

purposely : purposefully

Purposely means "intentionally" or, in the vernacular, "on purpose"; *purposefully* describes goal-oriented—purposeful—behavior.

shrink, shrank, shrunk

These are the standard forms for the present tense, past tense, and past participle of the verb *to shrink,* just like *sink/ sank/sunk, drink/drank/drunk, sing/sang/sung,* and *ring/ rang/rung.* That *shrunk* has gained some colloquial currency is clear from the title of the popular movie *Honey, I Shrunk the Kids.*

When asked why they gave their movie a purposely ungrammatical title, spokespeople for The Walt Disney Company replied that only *shrunk* is funny. *Honey, I Shrank the Kids,* they claimed, would not have seemed like a funny movie.

Nevertheless, using *shrunk, drunk, rung,* or *sung* as the simple past tense will never do if you want to be considered educated.

whether : whether or not

Whether will usually suffice without the *or not:* "I didn't know *whether* to laugh or cry." The *whether* should be replaced by *that* or *if* in expressions of doubt or uncertainty: "I wonder *if* she wants to marry him" is stronger than "I wonder *whether* she wants to marry him."

Do you "doubt if," "doubt that," or "doubt whether"? Again, try *that* first. Like the subjunctive, this one depends on the probability of the supposition: Use *that* if you are reasonably sure of your statement — in the positive or negative: "I doubt *that* he will come" or "There is no doubt *that* he'll come." (To say "There is no doubt *but that* he will come" is to say the opposite: i.e., "The only doubt is that he will come.")

Use *whether* if you are at all unsure: "I doubt *whether* I can get him to come." *I doubt if,* in this instance, is a less acceptable but perfectly colloquial replacement for *I doubt whether:* "I doubt *if* I can get him to come, but there's no harm in trying."

Or delete the subordinating conjunction altogether: "I doubt he'll come."

wrack : rack : wreck : wreak

You can *rack your brains* trying to figure out these *nerve-racking* words; the distinctions among them are enough to drive you to *wrack* and ruin, *wreak* havoc on you, and leave you a nervous *wreck.*

A *rack* is a frame or an instrument of torture. As a verb, *to rack* means "to stretch out or torture by stretching." *To wrack* is synonymous with *to wreck,* which is why you *rack* your brains and don't *wrack* them. *To wreak* is "to inflict a damaging blow," which is why you "wreak revenge."

Most of these, however, are clichés and should be avoided.

THIRTY-ONE WORDS WORD WATCHERS WATCH

Every word watcher has a list of words that are particularly annoying to see misused in print. The average reader often misses the misuse. Making the thirty-one distinctions that follow will not necessarily improve your writing, but, as William Safire says, it will improve your character.

burglary : robbery
callous : callus
canvas : canvass
casket : coffin
catsup : ketchup
childish : childlike
continually : continuously
cynic : skeptic
defective : deficient
forward : foreword
gourmet : gourmand : glutton
graduated : graduated from : was graduated from
gratified : grateful
hang : hung
lend : loan
lighted : lit

luxuriant : luxurious
oral : aural : verbal
pair of : pairs of
partially : partly
percent : percentage
pitiful : pitiable : piteous
prescribe : proscribe : prescription
prophecy : prophesy
ravish : ravage
sensuous : sensual
spoonsful : spoonfuls
stanch : staunch
try and : try to
whiskey : whisky
Xerox : photocopy

burglary : robbery

Not to get bogged down in legal distinctions, but *burglary* is breaking and entering with intent to commit a felony. It becomes *robbery* when threat or force is involved. In other words, it's burglary if no one's home.

callous : callus

You can be *callous* (an adjective) toward another person's feelings. You can *callous* (a verb) yourself toward that person. But you have a *callus* (a noun) on your ankle, which is *callused*.

canvas : canvass

A *canvas* (noun) is a piece of cloth. *To canvass* (verb) is to solicit or poll for opinions or votes, and the results are called a *canvass* (noun).

casket : coffin

Ambrose Bierce called *casket* a "needless euphemism affected by undertakers." *Casket* once meant a small, ornamented box, as it did when Shakespeare wrote the Casket Scene in *The Merchant of Venice*. Portia's suitors open small boxes filled with portraits; they do not open large boxes filled with corpses. Much to Bierce's displeasure, the genteel *casket* stuck, and schoolchildren ever since have thought *The Merchant of Venice* extremely morbid.

catsup : ketchup

The name of this seasoned tomato sauce is derived from the Malay *kuchap* and the Chinese *ke-tsiap;* for years the dictionaries have been spelling it *catsup* or, worse, *catchup*. Finally *The Random House Dictionary of the English Language, Second Edition, Unabridged* spelled it as we all have spelled it for years: *ketchup*.

childish : childlike

Childish is the insult, *childlike* the description.

continually : continuously

Continuously means "without interruption"; *continually* implies that an activity is ongoing. "A loquacious fellow who nevertheless finds time to eat and sleep is continually talking; but a great river flows continuously." (Ambrose Bierce, *Write It Right,* 1909).

cynic : skeptic

A *cynic* criticizes anyone and anything and assumes all motives to be base; a *skeptic* doubts the authenticity of an individual or object. A *cynic* is always *skeptical,* but a *skeptic* may retain some idealism.

A variant spelling, chiefly British, is *sceptic,* which looks as though it should be pronounced "septic."

defective : deficient

Defective refers to a defect, *deficient* to a deficiency. *Defective* pertains to quality, *deficient* to quantity.

forward : foreword

A *foreword* (literally, a "word before" the text) is a short introductory essay that comes before the table of contents and is usually by someone other than the author. Many writers and editors who should know better call it a *forward.*

gourmet : gourmand : glutton

The difference is a matter of degree: A *gourmet* is a connoisseur; a *gourmand* is an avid consumer; a *glutton* is an overindulger. Do not use *gourmand* as a fancy word for *gourmet; gourmet* is fancy enough.

graduated : graduated from : was graduated from

For those who wish to get these things right: You *graduate from* college; you don't *graduate* college—it's not a thing you can do *to* a college.

The old rule that you should say "I *was* graduated from college" is observed by few people today, kept alive only in author biographies on the dusty dust jackets of aging books.

gratified : grateful

Gratified means "pleased by"; *grateful* means "thankful for." "I am *gratified* by your attention and *grateful* for your help."

hang : hung

"Men are not hung," goes the old mnemonic; "pictures are." Juries are hung; men are not. Pictures and bells are hung; women and men are hanged.

lend : loan

This one is a question of sound: *Loan,* while a perfectly acceptable noun, is not a pretty verb. There's simply no poetry in "Friends, Romans, countrymen, *loan* me your ears" or "Neither a borrower nor a *loaner* be."

lighted : lit

Lighted is the preferred form for the past and past participle of *to light,* but *lit* is the more colloquial.

luxuriant : luxurious

Luxurious means "given to or characterized by luxury"; *luxuriant* means "abundant in growth": "The man with the luxuriant beard had a luxurious house with a luxuriant garden and a luxurious swimming pool."

oral : aural : verbal

Oral pertains to speaking or something that was spoken, *aural* to hearing or something that was heard. *Verbal* means "pertaining to words," which can be written, spoken, and heard. An agreement that is not written down is an *oral* agreement as well as a *verbal* agreement.

pair of : pairs of

The plural of *pair* is *pairs;* it has been for centuries: one pair of gloves, two pairs of gloves. *Two pair of gloves* is an archaism.

partially : partly

Ambrose Bierce called *partially* a "dictionary word, to swell the book." Nevertheless, it seems to have caught on. H. W. Fowler distinguishes between the two words by using *partly* as the opposite of *wholly,* and *partially* as the opposite of *completely.* But *partly* will do in most circumstances, and you might find that it's cleaner and brisker than *partially.*

percent : percentage

Use *percent* with a number. *Percentage* is preceded by an adjective: "A large *percentage* of the membership turned out for the meeting, over 80 *percent.*" Close up the *per* and the *cent,* and don't spell out the number.

The original form, *per centum* ("out of one hundred"), was abbreviated *per cent.* — with the period. By the beginning of the twentieth century the period had been dropped, but the words were still separate. Sometime after World War II the two words became one.

pitiful : pitiable : piteous

Piteous means "exhibiting suffering" ("a piteous moan"), whereas *pitiable* means "deserving of pity" ("a pitiable wretch"). *Pitiful* used to mean the same as *pitiable,* but it has come to have a pejorative meaning: Describing someone as a "pitiful wretch" expresses less compassion than using *pitiable.*

prescribe : proscribe : prescription

To prescribe means "to set down in writing." In medicine it means "to designate a treatment." *To proscribe* has a more specialized meaning: "to outlaw" or "to prohibit." Most often *prescribe* is the word meant.

People who confuse *prescription* with *subscription* are,

for the most part, people who as children had difficulty pronouncing the word *spaghetti*.

prophecy : prophesy

You *prophesy* (pronounced "sigh") a *prophecy* (pronounced "see"). With an *s* it's a verb, with a *c* a noun. There is no verb *to prophesize*.

ravish : ravage

To ravish is to transport with emotion—it can imply violent or nonviolent passion, up to and including the act of rape. *To ravage* means "to destroy"—it should be used only to convey violence. The two words should not be interchanged.

A short digression: A *radish* is a small red root eaten raw as a relish. In the Soviet Union before perestroika, *radish* was slang for someone who pretended to be a Communist— "Red on the outside, White on the inside"; the principle is like that of *Oreo* ("chocolate on the outside, vanilla on the inside"), African-American slang for "Uncle Tom."

sensuous : sensual

Up until the publication of *The Sensuous Woman* and *The Sensuous Man, sensual* was the more sexual of these two words. *Sensuous* merely meant "of or pertaining to the senses"—any or all of them. But best-selling books have a way of insinuating themselves into the public mind, and *sensuous* is now as carnal a word as *sensual*.

spoonful : spoonfuls

Put the plural at the end: "one *spoonful,* two *spoonfuls*"—because the word is spelled solid, unlike "one mother-in-law, two mothers-in-law" or "one attorney general, two attorneys general,'' which have the plural in the middle.

Some cookbooks still say ''two spoonsful,'' and some very old ones say ''two spoons full,'' but most cookbook editors today close up the phrase and eschew the center plural.

stanch : staunch

The words have come to be used interchangeably, but the old distinction was ''*Stanch* the bleeding, and remain *staunch.*''

try and : try to

''Try to remember,'' the song exhorts us. *Try and* should be used only in an expression like ''try and fail'' or ''try and try again,'' in which the verb *to try* is being joined to a synonymous or antonymic word. If the meaning is, as it usually is, ''to attempt to do something,'' *try* should be followed by the infinitive. Try to remember *that*.

whiskey : whisky

The Irish spell it *whiskey;* the English spell it *whisky.* Americans do as the Irish do, while the Scots and the Canadians side with the English.

While we're on the British Isles: *Scots* is the name of the dialect spoken in Scotland, and a *Scot* is someone who lives there. *Scottish* is the adjective, not *Scotch,* which is considered insulting by Scotsmen and Scotswomen. A *Briton* is an inhabitant of any of the British Isles, although try telling *that* to an Irishman. An *Englishman* or *-woman* is an inhabitant only of England. A *Breton* lives across the Channel, in Brittany.

Xerox : photocopy

Copyrighted names often fall into common usage and lose their initial capital letter, despite the wishes of the copyright holders. *Kerosene* is a prime example, as is *raisin bran;* both were originally copyrighted — and capitalized — terms but are so no longer.

In an attempt to protect their copyright and stave off the lowercase, Xerox launched an ad campaign to educate the public and instituted legal action against copyright infringers.

Writers interested in preserving the English language should help them. Use *photocopy* or even *copy* as the noun and the verb. Never decline or conjugate Xerox. (See pages 212–216 for a list of other trademarks and tricky names.)

Fax, on the other hand, has never been anyone's copyright. It's simply a shortened version of *facsimile.* You can decline it and conjugate it, and no one will complain or take you to court: I fax, you fax, he faxes; I faxed, I will fax, I am faxing.

TWO SLIPPERY SUFFIXES

-able : -ible
-ic : -ical

-able : -ible

There's no reliable way to know which of these two suffixes to use short of looking each one up or memorizing the vastly smaller list of *-ible* words. If it's any consolation, that's what copy editors do.

If you have any Latin, *-ible* is correct for Latinate words: *audible, visible, possible.* But Latinate words that came into

English via French take *-able: formidable, indispensable* (although *possible* in French is *possible*).

Most other words take *-able: comfortable, accountable, profitable*. Words that end in *e* drop it (*likable, notable,*) except for words that end in soft *c* or *g* sounds: *changeable, knowledgeable*.

-ic : -ical

Another difficult pair. In certain cases the two forms have different meanings: *Historic* means "having a place in history" while *historical* means "pertaining to the study of history": "a historic event" not "a historical event."

The suffixes work in the opposite way, however, for *economic* ("pertaining to economics") and *economical* ("frugal").

H. W. Fowler attempted to rid the language of all the *-ical*s in 1926. He was unable to do so, but his efforts have succeeded, to a certain extent, in scientific and technical usage: *botanic, geographic, philosophic,* and *ideologic* are all to be preferred to their longer *-ical*s.

TWO UNWITTING BRITICISMS

a : an
-ward : -wards

a : an

An historic event has been considered incorrect—in England and in America—since 1926, when it was first deplored by H. W. Fowler. It still persists in England, because they're used to it, and in America, among people, brought up on British literature, who think it more proper.

The only reason it was ever correct at all was that the *h* was unpronounced: *an 'istoric event.* The King James Bible, which was written back when *h*'s were unaspirated, is full of these *an*'s — and that is primarily why so many people think they are correct.

The rule is simple: Use *a* before all consonants (*a boy, a toy*) except the silent *h* (*an hour, an heiress,* ''Brutus is *an honorable* man'').

Also use *a* before aspirated vowels with *h, w,* or *y* sounds: *a humble abode, a once-in-a-lifetime experience, a European trip, a United Nations peacekeeping force.*

Use *an* only before a vowel with a vowel sound: *an alternate plan, an elegant style, an open mind.*

-ward : -wards

The suffix *-wards* is more often British: *Towards, afterwards,* and *backwards* are all Briticisms. In British English the *-s* denotes the adverbial form, and its absence denotes the adjectival form: The *backward* boy went *backwards.* In American English, both forms are more common without the final *-s.*

Nevertheless, *towards* is preferred by many American writers, most of whom simply think it looks better. The list of *towards* users, like the list of restrictive-*which* users, includes many great American writers. The choice is yours.

FIVE NONWORDS

alright
double entendre
momento

preventative
'till

alright

Are we all ready? There is no such word as *alright*. All right already?

double entendre

There is no such French expression as *double entendre*. There hasn't been for hundreds of years. The French expression for "double meaning" is *double entente*.

However, since Dryden, the British—who are fond of fracturing their French—have used the fake-French *entendre*. If you want to impress, hit that final *-te: double entente*.

momento

We will have *moments* to remember but *mementos* to remember them by. Some dictionaries say *momento* is a "variant spelling" for *memento*, but spelling it with an *o* is a memento mori for the English language.

preventative

There is no such medical term as *preventative*, although people have been making this mistake since the 1650s. The adjective and noun, as sanctioned by all major dictionaries as well as the American Medical Association style manual, are both *preventive*.

Query: If people have been making a mistake since the 1650s, why is it still a mistake?

'till

There is no such apostrophic contraction as *'till*. Think about it: What would the apostrophe stand for?

Till—with no apostrophe—has been a synonym for *until* since the sixteenth century. The old rule was to use *until* at the beginning of a sentence and *till* in the middle. (It's a nice rule, but . . . *why?*)

You can use *until* till the cows come home or *till* 'til hell freezes over, but the unnecessary apostrophe in *'till* is a sign of someone who dots *i*'s with little hearts—and promises to love you 'till the end of time.

A BONUS: FIVE WORDS NEVER TO MISSPELL

accommodate not **accomodate**
embarrass not **embarass**
harass not **harrass**
siege not **seige**
supersede not **supercede**

SEVEN

On Inspiration

Every writer is part editor, part creator. The proportions differ according to the person and the project. Some writers find it very hard to cut and clean their work; others can buff and shine and polish forever, sometimes editing the very life out of their original inspiration.

Anyone who has ever written knows that the desire to create can be, at times, delicate and shy and easily scared off. It can also be a powerful impulse, impossible to ignore. Learning to nurture the will to write along with the need to polish is difficult. The trick is in the timing: knowing when to let the creator loose and when the critic. The wise writer will create as much as possible while the inspiration is there. "Just get it down on paper," said editor Maxwell Perkins, "and then we'll see what to do with it."

There are two particularly difficult aspects of being a writer. The first is to get enough distance from your work to be able to forget who created it and how wonderful it was all meant to be. Looking at your writing with the cold and ruthless eye of a stranger is the only way to see what needs to be edited — edited *in* as well as out.

The second hard job is to be able to accept the bad writer within you, along with the good. The same

Charles Dickens who created *Great Expectations* collaborated on eight unreadable and unactable plays. It isn't reasonable to expect that every sentence we write will be brilliant or even that it will be good, at least not at its first appearance. "The first draft of anything," said Hemingway, "is shit."

If you can accept that, you will not be too discouraged when you reread your work and recognize your own bad writing. You will see it merely as a challenge to begin the next phase of being a writer: rewriting and editing. Writing is hard work; editing your own work is just as hard. It takes persistence and courage to root out the problems, word by word, idea by idea, beloved phrase by beloved phrase. It takes guts to get rid of what needn't be there.

INSPIRATION

The craft of writing can be learned and the technical skills perfected. But we do not all have it within ourselves to be brilliant, graceful, and imaginative writers or to write words that large audiences will want to read. For that you need talent and inspiration.

Many writers love talking about why and how they write. Rebecca West wrote "to find out about things." E. M. Forster said, "How do I know what I think until I see what I say?" Jorge Luis Borges wrote "to ease the passing of time." William Gass writes, he says, "because I hate. A lot. Hard."

Many writers are inspired by writing for someone in particular: Gabriel García Márquez said that "all books are written for your friends." Alfred North

Whitehead wrote for an audience of ten: "If others like it, that is clear gain. But to satisfy those ten is enough." John Updike writes for a "countryish teen-aged boy."

Others write entirely for themselves: Anthony Burgess's ideal reader is a "lapsed Catholic and failed musician, short-sighted, color-blind, auditorially biased, who has read the books I have read." E. B. White saw the "whole duty of a writer" as "to please and satisfy himself," and William Faulkner said, "Mine is the standard that has to be met."

Eudora Welty denied writing for her friends or for herself: "I write for *it*," she said, "for the sheer pleasure of *it*."

EIGHT WAYS TO GET STARTED

For many, there is no terror quite like facing a blank page. "Drawing blood" is the common metaphor. "Writing is easy," screenwriter Gene Fowler said. "All you do is sit staring at a blank sheet of paper until the drops of blood form on your forehead." Sportswriter Red Smith agreed. "There's nothing to writing. All you do is sit down at a typewriter and open a vein."

Writers use different tricks to get the writing going. Here are eight ways to get started and keep going.

Find yourself a quiet hour.

Think of writing as an activity for which you may have to act selfishly and protectively, a private habit that requires its own time and its own place. "All you need," said John Dos Passos, "is a room without any particular interruptions."

If you write at your job, try arriving an hour early; if you write at home, try waking up an hour earlier. Most people are too tired after a full day's work to begin a task as daunting as writing, although there are those who write best at night. Hemingway enjoyed working in the morning, "as soon after the first light as possible," he said. "There is no one to disturb you and it is cool or cold and you come to your work and warm as you write."

An hour of uninterrupted quiet time will yield the equivalent of several distracted hours. Find a time when no one else is around, in a room where no one will disturb you: a weekend afternoon in the attic or the basement, or an evening alone with your work spread out on the dining-room table. Turn off the television, and turn on the phone machine. "The ideal view for daily writing," wrote Edna Ferber, "is the blank brick wall of a cold-storage warehouse." Norman Mailer likes a room with a view, "preferably a long view," he says. "I prefer looking at the sea, or ships, or anything which has a vista to it."

Give yourself a time limit at first: forty-five minutes or an hour. That way, what lies ahead will seem less daunting. If you're lucky enough to have a whole day to yourself, plan to spend a three- or four-hour block of time. After that, have a meal, go for a walk, and then go back for another few hours. If the prospect of finding that many solitary hours seems unlikely, don't worry. Anthony Trollope said that three hours a day should produce "as much as a man ought to write."

Let your mind wander.

Just write. Don't worry about voice, tone, plot, or structure. Don't worry about grammar, usage, punctuation, or spelling. "Get black on white," said De Maupassant. Just write.

Write about breakfast or a dream you had. Write about what makes you happy. Write about what you hate. Write about anything that will get you writing. "The point," said Bernard Malamud, "is to get the pencil moving quickly."

Fill up a page with ramblings, but don't read them. Fill up another page. Write for the sheer sake of writing, with the express purpose of expressing your thoughts. Do not edit; do not judge; *show these pages to no one*. What you have written will not be clear or well organized—there will be time for that—but you will have written *something*.

Your goal should be similar to what the Victorians called "automatic writing." They believed that spirits could tell stories through our hands. Metaphysics aside, what you're after is your own spirit, free of the stress and anxiety that keep you from writing. Write freely and without embarrassment, and plan to come back later with all the technique you possess.

Do something physical.

If you cannot write, if you are blocked or anxiety ridden, do something physical that you can do without thinking. Go for a walk, a jog, or a bicycle ride — but not one so strenuous that you have to concentrate on it. Agatha Christie said that the best time for planning a book is "while you're doing the dishes." Cook or clean or do some gardening — but don't cook a six-course dinner for twelve, don't clean obsessively, and don't do the gardening with any pressure to do well. What you don't need is something else to be anxious about. Create a sense of calm that will encourage your imagination.

Understand the difference between simple procrastination and "productive procrastination." During simple procrastination you avoid the task at hand; during productive procrastination you meditate on it. Keep yourself busy, but put your mind to your writing. Don't force it, but, as in meditation, guide yourself gently to your subject, and, sooner or later, you will feel the need to sit down and write.

Write letters.

Writing a letter is the perfect warm-up to a productive writing session. People used to write letters regularly: to their parents, their lovers, their children, their friends. The practice instilled in them an ability to project their personality through the written word.

Use letter writing as practice. Try to convey information clearly and paint vivid pictures of what you are describing or feeling. Try to say on paper what would be difficult to say in person.

Perfecting techniques of self-expression in letters will not only help you in writing fiction, it will also give you powerful tools for many kinds of nonfiction. The more self-assurance you have about putting words on paper, the easier it will be for you to write at all.

Keep a diary or journal.

Write every day, no matter what. "Better far write twaddle or anything, *anything,*" Katherine Mansfield said, "than nothing at all."

Keep everything you write. Keeping a diary is a useful way to ingrain a daily writing habit. It can also be a good source of ideas for future writing. But diaries and journals are not for everyone. Most people begin them with a doomed burst of enthusiasm. For them, a better diary may be an envelope full of scraps of paper on which are caught fragments of life, expressed in the fiery language of the heat of the moment or the quiet reflection of the following morning. Some writers find they need the old-fashioned comfort of pen and paper; others form personal attachments to computers and printers. Computers are useful for keeping diaries and storing notes and drafts. Take the one good paragraph from yesterday's file and build a new version around it. But try not to get caught up in the mesmerizing world of technology; computers, like video games, can be hypnotic and addictive. Figuring out the disk operating system of your computer is a waste of a writing session.

Collecting your writing will give you a feeling of an ongoingness, of development. Carrying a pocket notebook in which you can jot down ideas, arguments, plot twists, and lines of dialogue will help you amass a body of work from which you can draw when inspiration fails.

Be honest.

If, like Dr. Seuss's Horton, you mean what you say and you say what you mean — and you say it simply and honestly — it will be well written.

All the rest is decoration.

Establish a routine.

Most productive writers, whether they are writing fiction or nonfiction, have disciplined themselves to write every day. They go to their writing as one would go to a job. If inspiration eludes them on a particular day or if they have a headache, they still go to work, often using the time for editing or polishing or planning what to write next.

If you have a routine of writing every weekend, four hours on Saturday, four hours on Sunday, think of yourself as having made a commitment to report to work eight hours a week. If something gets in the way of your working at one of these scheduled times, make up the hours as promptly as if you were employed by a hard taskmaster. You are.

If the taskmaster metaphor doesn't work for you, try thinking of writing time as a reward, a gift you can give yourself: a self-help regime, a path toward self-knowledge, and a creative outlet all in one. Think of it as exercise for your mind and your soul, as something you can work at that will make you stronger and wiser, as a habit to get into.

Not many people are lucky enough to be able to write full-time. The rest of us must carve out our writing time from our busy weeks. There are 168 hours in every week: 40 hours of work, 56 hours of sleep, and 21 hours of eating, leaving 51 hours a week — 7 hours and 17 minutes a day — for everything else. Anyone who really wants to can take an hour or two out of those 7 to write.

Writing is hard work, but doing it well, feeling satisfied, and being excited by your own words is one of life's sweetest experiences.

And when other people respond the way you hoped they would . . . ?

There is no greater joy.

Read.

The best way to learn good writing is to read good writers. Admire what they have done, and attempt it yourself. "I read in order to find out how to write," said A. S. Byatt. "Not the sort of reading to be done slacked down in cushions," said Edgar Allan Poe, "but set on a hard chair at a table with a pencil handy — the way the best reading is done, alert, combative, fit to argue and consider."

We are all part of a tradition of good writing. Learn to appreciate it, and dare to attempt it. As William Faulkner said:

Read, read, read. . . . Just like a carpenter who works as an apprentice and studies the master, read! You'll absorb it. Then write. If it is good, you'll find out. If it's not, throw it out the window.

APPENDIX I

The Random House Style Manual

The pages that follow are the guidelines used by Random House's copy editors and proofreaders in styling the work of our authors in matters such as punctuation, capitalization, italics, and the use of numbers. In many instances Random House style is not necessarily the same as that of any other publisher of books, magazines, or newspapers. Moreover, exceptions are made to this style from author to author and from book to book.

Good writing is good writing, even if it's badly punctuated. Bad writing is bad writing, even when immaculately punctuated. Some of the greatest Random House authors have used systems of punctuation entirely their own: James Joyce, William Faulkner, Gore Vidal, Anthony Burgess, James A. Michener, E. L. Doctorow, to name just a few.

All those writers are noted for their strong stylistic identities. It is inappropriate for most writing to call that kind of attention to itself. More often than not, a relatively anonymous style is the best way to get a message across. Anything nonstandard carries the possibility of what Strunk and White called the loss of a "fraction of the reader's attention." It is precisely to avoid that loss of attention that good authors rely on—and benefit from—good copy editors.

With each new author and each new book, Random House copy editors must choose which of the conventions will be applied and which ignored out of deference to the writer's style. More leeway is given to the author's preferences in fiction and first-person nonfiction than in third-person nonfiction. Especially in serious nonfiction that presents facts or ideas, the rules are applied more stringently.

Conventions are subject to the vagaries of time and fashion. The Constitution of the United States is filled with combinations of commas and dashes, colons and dashes, and periods and dashes. All of these were common in 1787:—all of them look odd today.* The writers of the Constitution capitalized words in the middle of sentences. Victorian writers used dashes and italics with abandon. Compounds that were formerly hyphenated are closed up now. What was common once now looks odd, and the styles we use today will probably look just as odd two hundred years from now, when the semicolon and the apostrophe may be extinct.

The conventions described in this appendix for styling punctuation, capitalization, italics, and numbers are those currently used for "trade" books—books for the general public—as set forth in the two industry standards, *Words into Type* and *The Chicago Manual of Style*.

If the author's choices aid the reader's comprehension of the material, they are the right choices. If those choices distract, confuse, or create the feeling

*See page 71.

that the writer is self-indulgent, they are the wrong choices. The aim is a simple and felicitous style. Some of these rules may seem wrong to you. Even so, know what is standard, and you can decide when to break the rules.

PUNCTUATION

Commas

Compound sentences and compound predicates
A comma should almost always be used in a compound sentence: two clauses, each containing its own subject and verb, separated by the conjunction *and, or, but, nor, for, so,* or *yet.*

• The sun came up on the storm-wracked world, and a new day dawned for all man- and womankind.

If one of the two clauses is short, the comma is optional.

• The sun came up and a new day dawned.

The comma should never separate a verb from its subject or a verb from its object.

• WRONG: The sun that shone that morning, was a brighter sun than had ever shone before.
• RIGHT: The sun that shone that morning was a brighter sun than had ever shone before.

The rule: A comma is usually necessary in a compound sentence only when the conjunction is followed by an independent clause with its own subject and verb.

- WRONG: The sun came up, and brought forth a new day.
- RIGHT: The sun came up and brought forth a new day.

However, if the sentence is particularly long or complicated, the comma may be used, although it is most often unnecessary.

- RIGHT: The sun came up on the storm-wracked, weary world, and brought forth a new day for all.
- RIGHT: The sun came up on the storm-wracked, weary world and brought forth a new day for all.

Adverbial phrases
Adverbial phrases at the beginnings of sentences are usually set off by commas:

- Filled with optimism, they set off for a new world.
- Having considered the alternatives, they opted to leave.

However, if the introductory adverbial phrase is shorter than five words, the comma is often not necessary:

- All in all it was the right thing to do.

A comma is not used after an introductory phrase that immediately precedes the verb and serves as the subject of the sentence:

• Leaving when they did was the best thing they could have done.

Following the verb, a dependent adverbial clause that is restrictive takes no comma:

• She refused to go unless her child could go with her.

However, if the clause is nonrestrictive, a comma is necessary:

• She agreed to leave for the new world, although her heart remained in the old.

If an adverbial clause or phrase comes between the subject and the verb, it is set off by commas:

• The child, sensing his mother's terror, clung to her skirts.

Restrictives and appositives
Commas set off nonrestrictive clauses, which usually begin with *which*.

• At the top of the hill is a large house, which was built long ago by someone named Jack.

Commas do not set off restrictive clauses, the ones that should begin with *that*.

- This is the house that Jack built.

Restrictive appositives do not take commas; nonrestrictive appositives do:

- Verdi's final opera, *Falstaff,* was based on Shakespeare's play *The Merry Wives of Windsor.*

Serial commas
Unless the writer objects strenuously, use the serial comma before the *and* in a series:

- red, white, and blue
- Wynken, Blynken, and Nod
- life, liberty, and the pursuit of happiness
- the sun, the moon, and the stars
- Shadrach, Meshach, and Abednego are the youths who escaped from the fiery furnace of Nebuchadnezzar.

Without the serial comma, it would be possible to misread this last sentence as telling Shadrach that Meshach and Abednego were the only youths to escape the fiery furnace.

Coordinate adjectives
Use a comma to separate coordinate adjectives — two or more adjectives that modify a noun — if each modifies the noun separately but not if the first modifies the compound of the second and the noun.

a faithful, devoted friend
a cold, gray winter day

> a merry old soul
> a dilapidated old barn

The rule: Use a comma if it could be replaced by the word *and*.

Interjections, transitions, and direct address
Use commas to set off transitional phrases, parenthetical comments, and other elements that interrupt the flow of the sentence, including dialogue and direct address:

- The concert, much to everyone's surprise, was a great success.
- "Shoot, sir, if you must," he said, "but shoot us both."
- It was, to say the least, a day for my memoirs.

Brief transitional words used as adverbs do not need to be set off by commas:

- The problem was indeed hers.
- The committee therefore decided to table the motion.

Use a comma after the exclamation *oh* but not after the vocative *O* (which is found only in archaic usages):

> "Oh, What a Beautiful Morning!"
> Oh, for Pete's sake!
> Oh, woe is me!
> O worthy king!

This comma may be dispensed with in certain phrases that have become as one:

> Yes sir!
> No sir!
> Oh boy!
> Oh yeah?
> Oh wow!

Semicolons

Use a semicolon to separate two independent clauses that are not joined by a conjunction.

- There was a long pause before he spoke again; the audience remained silent.

Use a semicolon before transitional adverbs like *however, nevertheless, besides, therefore,* and *indeed,* but a comma before coordinating conjunctions like *so* and *yet:*

- She entered the room with peals of laughter; however, there was no one there to greet her.
- There was nothing for us when we got there; nevertheless, we found something to eat.
- There was no one there to greet us, so we each took a seat and waited.

Use semicolons in series and in compound sentences in which individual elements are divided by commas.

- The trip would include visits to Albuquerque, New Mexico; Hackensack, New Jersey; and Ronkonkoma, New York.
- The chairman, who had been under attack for some time now, tried to call a brief recess; but his opponents, who were just beginning to gather steam, shouted him down and continued their barrage.

Do not use the semicolon before the *and* in a compound predicate or a compound sentence. In the first example below, the semicolon should be a comma, and in the second it should be deleted; both are from Gore Vidal's *Empire*.

- History had begun to lurch forward or backward or whatever; and Wilson was astride the beast, as old John Hay used to say of poor McKinley.
- Wilson held his cards above the lectern; and spoke as if to them.

Colons

Use a colon to introduce a clause or a series that amplifies or illustrates:

- The drive affords a delightful series of views: mountain vistas, rolling hills, lakefront beaches, and grazing cattle.
- The drive affords a delightful series of views: There are mountain vistas, rolling hills, lakefront beaches, and grazing cattle.

When a complete sentence follows a colon, a capital is recommended but not necessary.

Hyphens and Dashes

Dashes come in different sizes for different uses: small (hyphen: -), medium (en dash: –), and large (em dash: —).

Em dashes

Use an em dash to indicate a sudden break in continuity—a change in idea, a change in structure, a parenthetical comment, or an abrupt appositive. Note the use of the em dash with other marks of punctuation.

- If I knew then what I know now—and how I wish I did—I would not have gone.
- He had—how do you say it in English?—that certain "I do not know what."
- Excuse me, where do you think—? Hey! aren't you that guy from TV?
- "I can say with complete assurance" —and here he paused for effect—"that the murderer is among us."

Do not overuse em dashes. If the structure of the sentence is otherwise simple, commas can be used to set off appositives or brief parenthetical remarks. Parentheses can be used for more digressive comments.

Hyphens

The rules for hyphenated compounds are complex. They cover eleven pages in *The Chicago Manual of Style* and twelve pages in *Words into Type*. What follows are the general principles and some specific ex amples.

All contemporary dictionaries close up most words with prefixes and suffixes, including those with double consonants. Double vowels and triple consonants are usually hyphenated, except double *e*'s, which are usually closed up:

> preeminent
> antianxiety
> intra-atomic
> bell-like
> anti-inflammatory
> posttraumatic
> fossillike
> misspelled
> reelect

Some hyphens are used to avoid ambiguity or awkwardness.

> co-author
> co-op
> re-creation

The first is preferred to *coauthor;* the second would seem too much like a chicken coop, and the third, which means "something created anew," would be confused with the word *recreation,* which means what you do for fun.

Compound nouns usually are not hyphenated. There is no need for hyphens in the following compound nouns, although hyphens are used in the adjectival forms:

decision making	coal mining
decision maker	coal miner
decision-making process	coal-mining industry

Many of these compounds have become permanently closed (*childbearing, dressmaker, bookkeeeping*). A few of them are permanently hyphenated (*bird-watching*).

Dictionary consulting (no hyphen needed) is the only answer.

Compound adjectives are hyphenated if they come before the noun but not if they come after.

a well-known celebrity	the celebrity was well known
a so-called celebrity	so called because he is celebrated
a much-loved author	an author much loved by her fans

Some of these compound adjectives have become permanently hyphenated, whether before or after a noun.

a black-and-white photo	in color or in black-and-white
a half-baked scheme	his ideas were all half-baked
a matter-of-fact approach	his tone was matter-of-fact
an up-to-date manual	everything's up-to-date
a hard-boiled egg	that dame is sure hard-boiled

Never hyphenate a compound in which the first element is an adverb ending in *-ly*.

a badly written novel
a poorly bred child

> a smartly dressed gigolo
> an equally effective response

Never use a hyphen to connect a compound modifier to the noun it modifies.

> WRONG: a happy-birthday-card
> WRONG: a happy birthday-card
> RIGHT: a happy-birthday card

Certain open compounds are so firmly entrenched in the public's eye that it is distracting to hyphenate them when they come before a noun.

> a high school student
> an advertising agency employee
> a life insurance policy
> a grand jury investigation

When two colors are mixed they become a permanently hyphenated compound (*blue-green eyes, a dress that was lavender-blue*), but when the first is an adjective they should be left open: *bluish gray, reddish gold, the chiffon was lemon yellow*.

Let the possibility of distraction be your guide. If there is a possibility of the reader's misunderstanding on a single reading, use a hyphen. If you think there is little chance of confusion, omit the hyphen.

En dashes
En dashes are primarily used in typeset material to stand in for the word *to* in ranges of years, pages, and other numbers, as well as in boundaries and other linkages.

> pages 644–97
> 9:00 A.M.–5:00 P.M.
> Boston–Providence line
> blood–brain barrier
> the years 1801–1804
> Tuesday–Thursday

However, an en dash or hyphen should never replace the word *to* when the word *from* is used and should never replace the word *and*.

from 1989 to 1990   *not:* from 1989–90
between 1980 and 1990   *not:* between 1980–90

Use the en dash with an open, capitalized compound adjective or noun.

> pre–World War II movie
> a non–New Englander
> a Pulitzer Prize–winning author
> a New York–style cabdriver

Use a simple hyphen, not an en dash, if the compound that follows is hyphenated, unless two of the elements form a single unit.

* non-Spanish-speaking natives (the three parts are equal)
* Italian–Russian-Jewish ancestry (two elements form a unit)

NUMBERS

Spell out numbers one through one hundred and isolated, large round numbers (forty thousand people, twenty-four hundred, five million dollars). Spell out most numbers in dialogue, except when unwieldy. Spell out times of day (four o'clock, ten fifteen, eleven forty-two).

Some exceptions:

airplane model or flight numbers (a 747, flight 36)
years (1900, 2001)
votes and scores (with an en dash: 13–2)
military usage (5th Marine Regiment, 1500 hours)
sums of money in the millions, when they occur frequently ($5 million)

Always spell out a number at the beginning of a sentence, or rewrite the sentence to avoid.

Percents

Always use figures for percentages. Spell out and close up the word *percent* (45 percent, 10.9 percent, a 24 percent margin), except in tabular matter, where it is common to use the percent sign (45%). In dialogue, spell out both (''eighty-five percent,'' ''four and three quarters percent,'' ''a twenty-four-percent margin'').

Fractions

Do *not* hyphenate fractions as nouns (one third of the class, pour one fifth of the mixture). Hyphenate fractions as adjectives (a two-thirds majority, one-sixth inch wide).

Ages, Eras, and Street Addresses

Spell out the ages of people and things ("He is forty-five," "She is a forty-five-year-old").

Spell out and lowercase centuries ("in twentieth-century Spain," "in Spain in the twentieth century").

Spell out and lowercase decades of years ("a woman in her fifties," *but:* "the seventies" *or* "the 1970s"; "the 1970s and '80s").

Spell out and capitalize decades of streets ("He lives in the East Seventies").

Spell out and capitalize numbered streets from East First Street to One Hundredth Street. After that use cardinal or ordinal numbers ("She lives on West 101 Street" *or* ". . . 101st Street"). Lowercase the *s* if several streets are mentioned ("They live between East Tenth and East Eleventh streets").

CAPITALIZATION

Civil Titles

Capitalize official names of organizations but lowercase titles unless they come before names:

- President Fillmore said . . . (*but:* The president said . . .)
- The first lady said to the president . . .
- The State Department said . . .
- Secretary of State Cyrus Vance said . . . (*but:* The secretary of State [*or* state] said . . .)
- Pope John Paul II said . . . (*but:* The pope said . . .)

In Titles and Headings

Articles, coordinating conjunctions, and prepositions of four or fewer letters should be lowercased in titles and headings, along with the *to* in infinitives. Lowercase the following:

ARTICLES

a

an

the

COORDINATING CONJUNCTIONS

and

but

nor

or

PREPOSITIONS

as (when followed by a noun)

at

by

for

from

in

into

of
off
on
onto
out
to
up
with

Subordinating conjunctions, conjunctive adverbs, or other "little" words, like the verb *be,* should not be lowercased. Do *not* lowercase the following:

also
as (when followed by a verb)
be
if
than
that
then
thus
when

Capitalize adverbial prepositions that "belong" to a verb:

- "Hold On to Your Hat"
- "The Mafia Insider Who Turned on the Mob" (*not* ". . . Turned On the Mob" —unless you mean that the insider excited the mob)

Capitalize a preposition when it is the final word in a title:

- "Whom Shall I Turn To?"
- "What Am I Here For?"

SMALL CAPS

Use small caps—*not* caps and small caps—for signs, newspaper headlines, telegrams, and cables. Do not use them for acronyms or exclamatory remarks that should otherwise be set in full caps. Quotation marks are not necessary with small caps.

ELLIPSES

Use three ellipses to suggest a trailing off:

- "Well," she said, "the first thing I'd do is hire someone to shoot Mrs. Gary Cooper, and then . . ." (Dorothy Parker)

Use a period and three ellipses between complete sentences. The period is closed up on the left, but the ellipses are evenly spaced.

- Once upon a time there were three bears. . . . They lived happily ever after.

The final ellipsis is closed up to a closing quotation mark, but there is a space between a final ellipsis and an exclamation point or question mark.

- "Doctor? Is anything wrong with . . . ?"

If a complete sentence is connected to an incomplete sentence, use three ellipses and lowercase the first word of the sentence that follows.

• Had he lived . . . but he did not live, and Sophia Jane had hardly repaired the house she bought and got the orchard planted when she saw that, in her hands, the sugar refinery was going to be a failure. (Katherine Anne Porter)

FOREIGN ACCENTS AND DIACRITICAL MARKS

Use correct foreign accents on all words borrowed from Romance languages:

> naïveté
> résumé
> façade

Use Spanish inverted question marks and exclamation points when necessary:

> ¡La vía del tren subterráneo es peligrosa!

Use diacritical marks for German, Polish, and Hungarian, but do not use them with transliterated languages such as Russian, Chinese, and Japanese:

> Lech Wałęsa
> Nicolae Ceaușescu

POSSESSIVES

Use an apostrophe and an *s*, despite what you see in magazines or newspapers. Omitting the possessive *s* in the singular is *only* correct with names of classical or biblical derivation ending in *s:*

> Jesus'
> Xerxes'
> Moses'
> Mars'
> Achilles' heel (*but:* Achilles tendon)

All other names take the additional *s* in the singular.

> the countess's daughter
> George Burns's cigar
> the Burnses' house
> Mary and John's house (*but:* Mary's and John's houses)

ITALICS

Use italics or underline for titles of newspapers, journals, magazines, books, paintings, extended works of poetry, plays, movies, record albums, TV series, operas, oratorios, tone poems, or the official title of any extended work. Do not italicize the titles of short stories, short poems, songs, chapters, episodes of TV series, or short compositions; set them in quotation marks:

The New York Times
The King and I
Mona Lisa
Don Giovanni
Sesame Street
Paradise Lost
Abbey Road
"The Masque of the Red Death"
"Heroism"
"The Star-Spangled Banner"
"Chuckles the Clown"

Use italics for foreign words, unless those words have become part of the English language. Never italicize foreign proper names (people, places, organizations, churches, streets). Italicize words used as words and letters used as letters.

In newspaper and journal titles, italicize the word *the* and the city name only when this is done on the masthead. (See list below.)

Commas, colons, and semicolons should be set in the typeface (roman or italic, or boldface) of the preceding word.

Quotation marks, exclamation points, question marks, and parentheses are set according to the overall context of the sentence. (*"Hurrah!"* "I read it in *The New York Times*!")

NEWSPAPERS AND MAGAZINES

Italicize newspaper and magazine titles by their mast-heads:

the Albany (N.Y.)
  Times-Union
the *Atlantic Monthly* (now
  called *The Atlantic*)
the *Baltimore Sun*
The Boston Globe
the Chicago *Sun-Times*
the *Chicago Tribune*
*The Christian Science
  Monitor*
the Cleveland *Plain Dealer*
The Dallas Morning News
the Dallas *Times Herald*
The Denver Post
the *Los Angeles Times*
The Miami Herald
the *National Enquirer*
The New Republic
the New York *Daily News*
The New Yorker
New York magazine
the *New York Post*
*The New York Review of
  Books*

The New York Times
*The New York Times Book
  Review*
*The New York Times
  Magazine*
The Philadelphia Inquirer
the *San Francisco
  Chronicle*
the *San Francisco
  Examiner*
the *St. Louis Post-Dispatch*
the Tacoma (Wash.)
  Morning News Tribune
The Times (London) and
  The Sunday Times
  (London)
TV Guide
USA Today
The Village Voice
The Wall Street Journal
The Washington Post
Women's Wear Daily

MISCELLANEOUS TRADEMARKS, TITLES, AND TRICKY NAMES

A & P

Adrenalin (*but* adrenaline)

Alka-Seltzer

AmEx

Anheuser-Busch

Aqua-Fresh

Aqua-Lung

Aqua-Velva

Arm & Hammer

AstroTurf

AT&T

Automat

Band-Aid

BarcaLounger

Beefaroni

Ben-Gay

BFGoodrich

Bit-O-Honey

Breathalyzer

Bromo-Seltzer

Butter Buds

Cap'n Crunch

Cedars-Sinai

Chanel No. 5

Chap Stick

Chee·tos

Cheez Doodles

Cheez-It

Cheez Whiz

Chef Boyardee

CinemaScope

Cinerama

Citroën

Coca-Cola

CompuServe

Cool Whip

the Court of St. James's

Noël Coward

Cracker Jack

Cup·A·Soup

Cut-Rite

Day-Glo

Agnes de Mille

Cecil B. DeMille

Dentyne

Dewar's

Disneyland

Donahue, or the Phil Donahue show

Dr. Denton's

Dr Pepper

Dumpster

Dunkin' Donuts

Dustbuster

Elastoplast

Entenmann's

Etch-a-Sketch

FedEx
Fiberglas (*but* fiberglass)
Filofax
Fortnum & Mason
47 St. Photo
The Four Seasons
Freon
Frozfruit
Frusen Glädjé

Ginsu knife
Gone with the Wind (novel)
Gone With the Wind (film)
Good & Plenty
Good Morning America
Gore-Tex
Grauman's Chinese
　　Theatre
Guess!
Gulf + Western
Guns N' Roses

Häagen-Dazs
Handi-Wrap
Harley-Davidson
Harrods
Hawaiian Punch
Heimlich maneuver
Hermès
Hershey's Kisses
Hi-C
Hi-Dri
Hi-Liter

Horn & Hardart
Hula-Hoop

Instamatic

Jabba the Hutt
Jack Daniel's
Jacuzzi
Jazzercise
JCPenney
Jell-O
Jockey shorts
Johnnie Walker
Johnson's
Jujyfruits

Kahlúa
Kewpie doll
Nastassja Kinski
K mart
Ko-Rec-Type
Krazy Glue
K-Y

Lacoste
Land-Rover
LaserJet
*Late Night with David
　Letterman*
La-Z-Boy
Learjet
John le Carré
L'eggs
Levi's
Levolor

Lifebuoy

Life Savers

Light n' Lively

Liquid Paper

Liquid-Plumr

Little League

Lotus 1-2-3

Macintosh

MacNeil/Lehrer NewsHour

Magic Marker

M & M's

MasterCard

Mercedes-Benz

Miracle-Gro

Moby-Dick, Or, The Whale

Moët & Chandon

Monday Night Football

Moon Pie

Mouton Rothschild

Movietone

Moviola

Mr. Coffee

Mr. Goodwrench

Mr. Peanut

Mr. Potato Head

Mrs. Fields

Mrs. Paul's

Muzak

My*T*Fine

Nescafé

Nestlé

NFL Players Association

Novocain

NutraSweet

NyQuil

Ouija

Pac-Man

Parcheesi

Pepsi-Cola

Pepsi Light

Perrier-Jouët

Ping-Pong

Play-Doh

Plexiglas

Pop-Tart

Porsche

Portacrib

Porta-John

Porta Potti

Portosan

Post-It

Q-Tips

Quaalude

Ragú

Rapifax

Ray-Ban

ReaLemon

Record-A-Call

Reddi Wip

Rolls-Royce

Rolodex

SaladShooter

S & P 500

Sani-Flush

Sara Lee

Saran Wrap

Savile Row

Scotch tape

ScotTissue

Screen Actors Guild

Seeing Eye

7-Eleven

7UP

Shake 'n Bake

Sheetrock

Sargent Shriver

Simonīz

Skilsaw

Smell-O-Vision

Sno Balls

Sno-Cat

Sno-Kone

Snooz Alarm

SpaghettiOs

Spam

Speedo

Spic and Span

Spray 'n Vac

Spray 'n Wash

StairMaster

Stop & Shop

Styrofoam [NOTE: packing
   material only; cups and

serving items are *not*
made of Styrofoam]

Super Ball

Super Bowl

Super Glue

Sweet'n Low

Swissair

TelePrompTer

Texas A&M University

Thermopane

3-In-One

3M

3 Musketeers

Time & Life Building

Tinkertoy

the *Today* show

Toll-House

*The Tonight Show (Starring
   Johnny Carson)*

Top-Sider

Trivial Pursuit

Harry S Truman (no period
   after the *S*)

Twentieth Century–Fox

the "21" Club

Ty-D-Bol

U-Bahn

U-Haul

USAir

Uzi

V-8

Velcro

Vistavision

Vitaphone

Vitascope

VO5

Walgreens

Walt Disney World

Warner Bros., Warners

WordPerfect

X-Acto

Xerox (always capped,
   never a verb)

Yoo-Hoo

Ziploc

APPENDIX II

A Well-Written Story

"The Masque of the Red Death"
by Edgar Allan Poe

exposition The "Red Death" had long devastated the country. No pestilence had ever been so fatal, or so hideous. Blood was its Avatar and its seal—the redness and the horror of blood. There were sharp pains, and sudden dizziness, and then profuse bleeding at the pores, with dissolution. The scarlet stains upon the body and especially upon the face of the victim, were the pest ban which shut him out from the aid and from the sympathy of his fellowmen. And the whole seizure, progress, and termination of the disease, were the incidents of half an hour.

But the Prince Prospero was happy and dauntless and sagacious. When his dominions were half depopulated, he summoned to his presence a thousand hale and lighthearted friends from among the knights and dames of his court, and with these retired to the deep seclusion of one of his castellated abbeys. This was an extensive and magnificent structure, the creation of the prince's own eccentric yet august taste. A strong and lofty wall girdled it in. This wall had gates of iron. The courtiers, having entered, brought furnaces and massy hammers and welded the bolts. They resolved to leave means neither of ingress nor egress to the sudden impulses of despair or of frenzy from within. The abbey was amply provisioned. With such precautions the courtiers might bid defiance to contagion. The external world could take care of itself. In the meantime it was folly to grieve, or to think. The prince had provided all the appliances of pleasure. There were buffoons, there were improvisatori, there were ballet-dancers, there were musicians, there was Beauty, there was wine. All these and security were within. Without was the "Red Death."

It was toward the close of the fifth or sixth month of his seclusion, and while the pestilence raged most furiously abroad, that the Prince Prospero entertained his thousand friends at a masked ball of the most unusual magnificence.

precipitating event   It was a voluptuous scene, that masquerade. But first let me tell of the rooms in which it was held. There were seven—an imperial suite. In many palaces, however, such suites form a long and straight vista, while the folding doors slide back nearly to the walls on either hand, so that the view of the whole extent is scarcely impeded. Here the case was very different; as might have been expected from the duke's love of the *bizarre*. The apartments were so irregularly disposed that the vision embraced but little more than one at a time. There was a sharp turn at every twenty or thirty yards, and at each turn a novel effect. To the right and left, in the middle of each wall, a tall and narrow Gothic window looked out upon a closed corridor which pursued the windings of the suite. These windows were of stained glass whose color varied in accordance with the prevailing hue of the decorations of the chamber into which it opened. That at the eastern extremity was hung, for example, in blue—and vividly blue were its windows. The second chamber was purple in its ornaments and tapestries, and here the panes were purple. The third was green throughout, and so were the casements. The fourth was furnished and lighted with orange — the fifth with white — the sixth with violet. The seventh apartment was closely shrouded in black velvet tapestries that hung all over the ceiling and down the walls, falling in heavy folds upon a carpet of the same material and hue. But in this chamber only, the color of the windows failed to correspond with the decorations. The panes here were scarlet — a deep blood color. Now in no one of the seven apartments was there any lamp or candelabrum, amid the profusion of golden ornaments that lay scattered to and fro or depended from the roof. There was no light of any kind emanating from lamp or candle within the suite of chambers. But in the corridors that followed the suite, there stood, opposite to each window, a heavy tripod, bearing a brazier of fire, that projected its rays through the tinted glass and so glaringly illumined the room. And thus were produced a multitude of gaudy and fantastic appearances. But in the western or black chamber the effect of the fire-light that streamed upon the dark hangings through the blood-tinted panes was ghastly in the extreme, and produced so wild a look upon the countenances of those who entered, that there were few of the company bold enough to set foot within its precincts at all.

It was in this apartment, also, that there stood against the western wall, a gigantic clock of ebony. Its pendulum swung to and fro with a dull, heavy, monotonous clang; and when the minute-hand made the circuit of the face, and the hour was to be stricken, there came from the brazen lungs of the clock a sound which was clear and loud and deep and exceedingly musical, but of so peculiar a note and emphasis that, at each lapse of an hour, the musicians of the orchestra were constrained to pause, momentarily, in their performance, to hearken to the sound; and thus the waltzers perforce ceased their evolutions; and there was a brief disconcert of the whole gay company; and, while the chimes of the clock yet rang, it was observed that the giddiest grew pale, and the more aged and sedate passed their hands over their brows as if in confused revery or meditation. But when the echoes had fully ceased, a light laughter at once pervaded the assembly; the musicians looked at each other and smiled as if at their own nervousness and folly, and made whispering vows, each to the other, that the next chiming of the clock should produce in them no similar emotion; and then, after the lapse of sixty minutes (which embrace three thousand and six hundred seconds of the Time that flies), there came yet another chiming of the clock, and then were the same disconcert and tremulousness and meditation as before.

But, in spite of these things, it was a gay and magnificent revel. The tastes of the duke were peculiar. He had a fine eye for colors and effects. He disregarded the *decora* of mere fashion. His plans were bold and fiery, and his conceptions glowed with barbaric lustre. There are some who would have thought him mad. His followers felt that he was not. It was necessary to hear and see and touch him to be *sure* that he was not.

He had directed, in great part, the movable embellishments of the seven chambers, upon occasion of this great *fête*; and it was his own guiding taste which had given character to the masqueraders. Be sure they were grotesque. There were much glare and glitter and piquancy and phantasm—much of what has been since seen in "Hernani." There were arabesque figures with unsuited limbs and appointments. There were delirious fancies such as the madman fashions. There were much of the beautiful, much of the wanton, much of the *bizarre,* something of the terrible, and not a little of that which might have excited disgust. To and fro in the seven chambers there stalked, in fact, a multitude of dreams. And these — the dreams — writhed in and about, taking hue from the rooms, and causing the wild music of the orchestra to seem as the echo of their steps. And, anon, there strikes the ebony clock which stands in the hall of the velvet. And then, for a moment, all is still, and all is silent save the voice of the clock. The dreams are stiff-frozen as they stand. But the echoes of the chime die away — they have endured but an instant — and a light, half-subdued laughter floats after them as they depart. And now again the music swells, and the dreams live, and writhe to and fro more merrily than ever, taking hue from the many-tinted windows through which stream the rays from the tripods. But to the chamber which lies most westwardly of the seven there are now none of the maskers who venture; for the night is waning away; and there flows a ruddier light through the blood-colored panes; and the blackness of the sable drapery appals; and to him whose foot falls upon the sable carpet, there comes from the near clock of ebony a muffled peal more solemnly emphatic than any which reaches *their* ears who indulge in the more remote gaieties of the other apartments.

complication But these other apartments were densely crowded, and in them beat feverishly the heart of life. And the revel went whirlingly on, until at length there commenced the sounding of midnight upon the clock. And then the music ceased, as I have told; and the evolutions of the waltzers were quieted; and there was an uneasy cessation of all things as before. But now there were twelve strokes to be sounded by the bell of the clock; and thus it happened, perhaps that more of thought crept, with more of time, into the meditations of the thoughtful among those who revelled. And thus too, it happened, perhaps, that before the last echoes of the last chime had utterly sunk into silence, there

were many individuals in the crowd who had found leisure
to become aware of the presence of a masked figure which
had arrested the attention of no single individual before. And
the rumor of this new presence having spread itself whisper-
ingly around, there arose at length from the whole company
a buzz, or murmur, expressive of disapprobation and surprise—then, finally, of terror, of horror, and of disgust.

In an assembly of phantasms such as I have painted, it
may well be supposed that no ordinary appearance could
have excited such sensation. In truth the masquerade license
of the night was nearly unlimited; but the figure in question
had out-Heroded Herod, and gone beyond the bounds of
even the prince's indefinite decorum. There are chords in the
hearts of the most reckless which cannot be touched without
emotion. Even with the utterly lost, to whom life and death
are equally jests, there are matters of which no jest can be
made. The whole company, indeed, seemed now deeply to
feel that in the costume and bearing of the stranger neither
wit nor propriety existed. The figure was tall and gaunt, and
shrouded from head to foot in the habiliments of the grave.
The mask which concealed the visage was made so nearly to
resemble the countenance of a stiffened corpse that the closest scrutiny must have had difficulty in detecting the cheat.
And yet all this might have been endured, if not approved,
by the mad revellers around. But the mummer had gone so
far as to assume the type of the Red Death. His vesture was
dabbled in *blood*—and his broad brow, with all the features
of the face, was besprinkled with the scarlet horror.

When the eyes of Prince Prospero fell upon this spectral
image (which, with a slow and solemn movement, as if more
fully to sustain its *rôle,* stalked to and fro among the waltzers) he was seen to be convulsed, in the first moment with a

strong shudder either of terror or distaste; but, in the next, his brow reddened with rage.

crisis   "Who dares"—he demanded hoarsely of the courtiers who stood near him—"who dares insult us with this blasphemous mockery? Seize him and unmask him—that we may know whom we have to hang, at sunrise, from the battlements!"

It was in the eastern or blue chamber in which stood the Prince Prospero as he uttered these words. They rang throughout the seven rooms loudly and clearly, for the prince was a bold and robust man, and the music had become hushed at the waving of his hand.

It was in the blue room where stood the prince, with a group of pale courtiers by his side. At first, as he spoke, there was a slight rushing movement of this group in the direction of the intruder, who, at the moment was also near at hand, and now, with deliberate and stately step, made closer approach to the speaker. But from a certain nameless awe with which the mad assumptions of the mummer had inspired the whole party, there were found none who put forth hand to seize him; so that, unimpeded, he passed within a yard of the prince's person; and, while the vast assembly, as if with one impulse, shrank from the centres of the rooms to the walls, he made his way uninterruptedly, but with the same solemn and measured step which had distinguished him from the first, through the blue chamber to the purple—through the purple to the green—through the green to the orange—through this again to the white—and even thence to the violet, ere a decided movement had been made to arrest him. It was then, however, that the Prince Prospero, maddening with rage and the shame of his own momentary cowardice, rushed hurriedly through the six chambers, while none followed him on account of a deadly terror that had seized upon

all. He bore aloft a drawn dagger, and had approached, in rapid impetuosity, to within three or four feet of the retreat-
climax   ing figure, when the latter, having attained the ex-
tremity of the velvet apartment, turned suddenly and confronted his pursuer. There was a sharp cry — and the dagger dropped gleaming upon the sable carpet, upon which, instantly afterward, fell prostrate in death the Prince Prospero. Then, summoning the wild courage of despair, a throng of the revellers at once threw themselves into the black apartment, and, seizing the mummer, whose tall figure stood erect and motionless within the shadow of the ebony clock, gasped in unutterable horror at finding the grave cerements and corpse-like mask, which they handled with so violent a rudeness, untenanted by any tangible form.

resolution   And now was acknowledged the presence of the
Red Death. He had come like a thief in the night. And one by one dropped the revellers in the blood-bedewed halls of their revel, and died each in the despairing posture of his fall. And the life of the ebony clock went out with that of the last of the gay. And the flames of the tripods expired. And Darkness and Decay and the Red Death held illimitable dominion over all.

APPENDIX III

A Well-Written Essay

"Character"
by Ralph Waldo Emerson

¶1   I have read that those who listened to Lord Chatham felt that there was something finer in the man, than anything which he said. It has been complained of our brilliant English historian of the French Revolution, that when he has told all his facts about Mirabeau, they do not justify his estimate of his genius. The Gracchi, Agis, Cleomenes, and others of Plutarch's heroes, do not in the record of facts equal their own fame. Sir Philip Sidney, the Earl of Essex, Sir Walter Raleigh, are men of great figure, and of few deeds. We cannot find the smallest part of the personal weight of Washington, in the narrative of his exploits. The authority of the name of Schiller is too great for his books. This inequality of the reputation to the works or the anecdotes, is not accounted for by saying that the reverberation is longer than the thunder-clap; but somewhat resided in these men which begot an expectation that outran all their performance. The largest part of their power was latent.

thesis   This is that which we call Character, — a reserved force which acts directly by presence, and without means. It is conceived of as a certain undemonstrable force, a Familiar or Genius, by whose impulses the man is guided, but whose counsels he cannot impart; which is company for him, so

that such men are often solitary, or if they chance to be social, do not need society, but can entertain themselves very
well alone. The purest literary talent appears at one time
great, at another time small, but character is of a stellar and
undiminishable greatness. What others effect by talent or by
eloquence, this man accomplishes by some magnetism.
"Half his strength he put not forth." His victories are by
demonstration of superiority, and not by crossing of bayo-
nets. He conquers, because his arrival alters the face of affairs. ' "O Iole! how did you know that Hercules was a
god?" "Because," answered Iole, "I was content the moment my eyes fell on him. When I beheld Theseus, I desired
that I might see him offer battle, or at least guide his horses
in the chariot-race; but Hercules did not wait for a contest;
he conquered whether he stood, or walked, or sat, or whatever thing he did." ' Man, ordinarily a pendant to events,
only half attached, and that awkwardly, to the world he lives
in, in these examples appears to share the life of things, and
to be an expression of the same laws which control the tides
and the sun, numbers and quantities.

¶2   But to use a more modest illustration, and nearer home,
I observe, that in our political elections, where this element, if it appears at all, can only occur in its coarsest form,
we sufficiently understand its incomparable rate. The people

counterarguments   know that they need in their representative
much more than talent, namely, the power
to make his talent trusted. They cannot come at their ends by
sending to Congress a learned, acute, and fluent speaker, if
he be not one, who, before he was appointed by the people to
represent them, was appointed by Almighty God to stand for
a fact,—invincibly persuaded of that fact in himself,—so
that the most confident and the most violent persons learn
that here is resistance on which both impudence and terror

are wasted, namely, faith in a fact. The men who carry their points do not need to inquire of their constituents what they should say, but are themselves the country which they represent: nowhere are its emotions or opinions so instant and true as in them; nowhere so pure from a selfish infusion. The constituency at home hearkens to their words, watches the color of their cheek, and therein, as in a glass, dresses its own. Our public assemblies are pretty good tests of manly force. Our frank countrymen of the west and south have a taste for character, and like to know whether the New Englander is a substantial man, or whether the hand can pass through him.

¶3 The same motive force appears in trade. There are geniuses in trade, as well as in war, or the state, or letters; and the reason why this or that man is fortunate, is not to be told. It lies in the man: that is all anybody can tell you about it. See him, and you will know as easily why he succeeds, as, if you see Napoleon, you would comprehend his fortune. In the new objects we recognize the old game, the habit of fronting the fact, and not dealing with it at second hand, through the perceptions of somebody else. Nature seems to authorize trade, as soon as you see the natural merchant, who appears not so much a private agent, as her factor and Minister of Commerce. His natural probity combines with his insight into the fabric of society, to put him above tricks, and he communicates to all his own faith, that contracts are of no private interpretation. The habit of his mind is a reference to standards of natural equity and public advantage; and he inspires respect, and the wish to deal with him, both for the quiet spirit of honor which attends him, and for the intellectual pastime which the spectacle of so much ability affords. This immensely stretched trade, which makes the capes of the Southern Ocean his wharves, and the Atlantic Sea his familiar port, centres in his brain only; and nobody in the universe can make his place good. In his parlor, I see very well that he has been at hard work this morning, with that knitted brow, and that settled humor, which all his desire to be courteous cannot shake off. I see plainly how many firm acts have been done; how many valiant *noes* have this day been spoken, when others would have uttered ruinous *yeas*. I see, with the pride of art, and skill of masterly arithmetic and power of remote combination, the consciousness of being an agent and playfellow of the original laws of the world. He too believes that none can supply him, and that a man must be born to trade, or he cannot learn it.

¶4   This virtue draws the mind more, when it appears in action to ends not so mixed. It works with most energy in the smallest companies and in private relations. In all cases, it is an extraordinary and incomputable agent. The excess of physical strength is paralyzed by it. Higher natures overpower lower ones by affecting them with a certain sleep. The faculties are locked up, and offer no resistance. Perhaps that is the universal law. When the high cannot bring up the low to itself, it benumbs it, as man charms down the resistance of the lower animals. Men exert on each other a similar occult power. How often has the influence of a true master realized all the tales of magic! A river of command seemed to run down from his eyes into all those who beheld him, a torrent of strong sad light, like an Ohio or Danube, which pervaded them with his thoughts, and colored all events with the hue of his mind. ''What means did you employ?'' was the question asked of the wife of Concini, in regard to her treatment of Mary of Medici; and the answer was, ''Only that influence which every strong mind has over a weak one.'' Cannot Caesar in irons shuffle off the irons, and transfer them to the person of Hippo or Thraso the turnkey? Is an iron handcuff so immutable a bond? Suppose a slaver on the coast of Guinea should take on board a gang of negroes, which should contain persons of the stamp of Toussaint L'Ouverture: or, let us fancy, under these swarthy masks he has a gang of Washingtons in chains. When they arrive at Cuba, will the relative order of the ship's company be the same? Is there nothing but rope and iron? Is there no love, no reverence? Is there never a glimpse of right in a poor slave-captain's mind; and cannot these be supposed available to break, or elude, or in any manner overmatch the tension of an inch or two of iron ring?

¶5

body

This is a natural power, like light and heat, and all nature coöperates with it. The reason why we feel one man's presence, and do not feel another's, is as simple as gravity. Truth is the summit of being: justice is the application of it to affairs. All individual natures stand in a scale, according to the purity of this element in them. The will of the pure runs down from them into other natures, as water runs down from a higher into a lower vessel. This natural force is no more to be withstood, than any other natural force. We can drive a stone upward for a moment into the air, but it is yet true that all stones will forever fall; and whatever instances can be quoted of unpunished theft, or of a lie which somebody credited, justice must prevail, and it is the privilege of truth to make itself believed. Character is this moral order seen through the medium of an individual nature. An individual is an encloser. Time and space, liberty and necessity, truth and thought, are left at large no longer. Now, the universe is a close or pound. All things exist in the man tinged with the manners of his soul. With what quality is in him, he infuses all nature that he can reach; nor does he tend to lose himself in vastness, but, at how long a curve soever, all his regards return into his own good at last. He

animates all he can, and he sees only what he animates. He
encloses the world, as the patriot does his country, as a material basis for his character, and a theatre for action. A healthy
soul stands united with the Just and the True, as the magnet
arranges itself with the pole, so that he stands to all behold-
ers like a transparent object betwixt them and the sun, and
whoso journeys towards the sun, journeys towards that person. He is thus the medium of the highest influence to all
who are not on the same level. Thus, men of character are
the conscience of the society to which they belong.

¶6   The natural measure of this power is the resistance of
circumstances. Impure men consider life as it is reflected in opinions, events, and persons. They cannot see the
action, until it is done. Yet its moral element pre-existed in
the actor, and its quality as right or wrong, it was easy to
predict. Everything in nature is bipolar, or has a positive and
negative pole. There is a male and a female, a spirit and a
fact, a north and a south. Spirit is the positive, the event is
the negative. Will is the north, action the south pole. Character may be ranked as having its natural place in the north. It
shares the magnetic currents of the system. The feeble souls
are drawn to the south or negative pole. They look at the
profit or hurt of the action. They never behold a principle
until it is lodged in a person. They do not wish to be lovely,
but to be loved. The class of character like to hear of their
faults: the other class do not like to hear of faults; they worship events; secure to them a fact, a connexion, a certain
chain of circumstances, and they will ask no more. The hero
sees that the event is ancillary: it must follow *him*. A given
order of events has no power to secure to him the satisfaction
which the imagination attaches to it; the soul of goodness
escapes from any set of circumstances, whilst prosperity belongs to a certain mind, and will introduce that power and

victory which is its natural fruit, into any order of events. No change of circumstances can repair a defect of character. We boast our emancipation from many superstitions; but if we have broken any idols, it is through a transfer of the idolatry. What have I gained, that I no longer immolate a bull to Jove, or to Neptune, or a mouse to Hecate; that I do not tremble before the Eumenides, or the Catholic Purgatory, or the Calvinistic Judgment-day, — if I quake at opinion, the public opinion, as we call it; or at the threat of assault, or contumely, or bad neighbors, or poverty, or mutilation, or at the rumor of revolution, or of murder? If I quake, what matters it what I quake at? Our proper vice takes form in one or another shape, according to the sex, age, or temperament of the person, and, if we are capable of fear, will readily find terrors. The covetousness or the malignity which saddens me, when I ascribe it to society, is my own. I am always environed by myself. On the other part, rectitude is a perpetual victory, celebrated not by cries of joy, but by serenity, which is joy fixed or habitual. It is disgraceful to fly to events for confirmation of our truth and worth. The capitalist does not run every hour to the broker, to coin his advantages into current money of the realm; he is satisfied to read in the quotations of the market, that his stocks have risen. The same transport which the occurrence of the best events in the best order would occasion me, I must learn to taste purer in the perception that my position is every hour meliorated, and does already command those events I desire. That exultation is only to be checked by the foresight of an order of things so excellent, as to throw all our prosperities into the deepest shade.

¶7   The face which character wears to me is self-sufficingness. I revere the person who is riches; so that I cannot think of him as alone, or poor, or exiled, or unhappy, or a client, but as perpetual patron, benefactor, and beatified man. Character is centrality, the impossibility of being displaced or overset. A man should give us a sense of mass. Society is frivolous, and shreds its day into scraps, its conversation into ceremonies and escapes. But if I go to see an ingenious man, I shall think myself poorly entertained if he give me nimble pieces of benevolence and etiquette; rather he shall stand stoutly in his place, and let me apprehend, if it were only his resistance; know that I have encountered a new and positive quality; — great refreshment for both of us. It is much, that he does not accept the conventional opinions and practices. That nonconformity will remain a goad and remembrancer, and every inquirer will have to dispose of him, in the first place. There is nothing real or useful that is not a seat of war. Our houses ring with laughter and personal and critical gossip, but it helps little. But the uncivil, unavailable man, who is a problem and a threat to society, whom it cannot let pass in silence, but must either worship or hate, — and to whom all parties feel related, both the leaders of opinion, and the obscure and eccentric, — he helps; he puts America and Europe in the wrong, and destroys the skepticism which says, 'man is a doll, let us eat and drink, 'tis the best we can do,' by illuminating the untried and unknown. Acquiescence in the establishment, and appeal to the public, indicate infirm faith, heads which are not clear, and which must see a house built, before they can comprehend the plan of it. The wise man not only leaves out of his thought the many, but leaves out the few. Fountains, fountains, the self-moved, the absorbed, the commander because he is commanded, the assured, the primary, — they are good; for these announce the instant presence of supreme power.

¶8   Our action should rest mathematically on our substance. In nature, there are no false valuations. A pound of water in the ocean-tempest has no more gravity than in a midsummer pond. All things work exactly according to their quality, and according to their quantity; attempt nothing they cannot do, except man only. He has pretension: he wishes and attempts things beyond his force. I read in a book of English memoirs, ''Mr. Fox (afterwards Lord Holland) said, he must have the Treasury; he had served up to it, and would have it.'' — Xenophon and his Ten Thousand were quite equal to what they attempted, and did it; so equal, that it was not suspected to be a grand and inimitable exploit. Yet there stands that fact unrepeated, a high-water-mark in military history. Many have attempted it since, and not been equal to it. It is only on reality, that any power of action can be based. No institution will be better than the institutor. I knew an amiable and accomplished person who undertook a practical reform, yet I was never able to find in him the enterprise of love he took in hand. He adopted it by ear and by the understanding from the books he had been reading. All his action was tentative, a piece of the city carried out into the fields, and was the city still, and no new fact, and could not inspire enthusiasm. Had there been something latent in the man, a terrible undemonstrated genius agitating and embarrassing his demeanor, we had watched for its advent. It is not enough that the intellect should see the evils, and their remedy. We shall still postpone our existence, nor take the ground to which we are entitled, whilst it is only a thought, and not a spirit that incites us. We have not yet served up to it.

¶9 These are properties of life, and another trait is the notice of incessant growth. Men should be intelligent and earnest. They must also make us feel, that they have a controlling happy future, opening before them, which sheds a splendor on the passing hour. The hero is misconceived and misreported: he cannot therefore wait to unravel any man's blunders: he is again on his road, adding new powers and honors to his domain, and new claims on your heart, which will bankrupt you, if you have loitered about the old things, and have not kept your relation to him, by adding to your wealth. New actions are the only apologies and explanations of old ones, which the noble can bear to offer or to receive. If your friend has displeased you, you shall not sit down to consider it, for he has already lost all memory of the passage, and has doubled his power to serve you, and, ere you can rise up again, will burden you with blessings.

¶10   We have no pleasure in thinking of a benevolence that is only measured by its works. Love is inexhaustible, and if its estate is wasted, its granary emptied, still cheers and enriches, and the man, though he sleep, seems to purify the air, and his house to adorn the landscape and strengthen the laws. People always recognize this difference. We know who is benevolent, by quite other means than the amount of subscription to soup-societies. It is only low merits that can be enumerated. Fear, when your friends say to you what you have done well, and say it through; but when they stand with uncertain timid looks of respect and half-dislike, and must suspend their judgment for years to come, you may begin to hope. Those who live to the future must always appear selfish to those who live to the present. Therefore it was droll in the good Riemer, who has written memoirs of Goethe, to make out a list of his donations and good deeds, as, so many hundred thalers given to Stilling, to Hegel, to Tischbein: a lucrative place found for Professor Voss, a post under the Grand Duke for Herder, a pension for Meyer, two professors recommended to foreign universities, &c. &c. The longest list of specifications of benefit, would look very short. A man is a poor creature, if he is to be measured so. For, all these, of course, are exceptions; and the rule and hodiernal life of a good man is benefaction. The true charity of Goethe is to be inferred from the account he gave Dr. Eckermann, of the way in which he had spent his fortune. "Each bonmot of mine has cost a purse of gold. Half a million of my own money, the fortune I inherited, my salary, and the large income derived from my writings for fifty years back, have been expended to instruct me in what I now know. I have besides seen," &c.

¶11   I own it is but poor chat and gossip to go to enumerate traits of this simple and rapid power, and we are painting the lightning with charcoal; but in these long nights and vacations, I like to console myself so. Nothing but itself can copy it. A word warm from the heart enriches me. I surrender at discretion. How death-cold is literary genius before this fire of life! These are the touches that reanimate my heavy soul, and give it eyes to pierce the dark of nature. I find, where I thought myself poor, there was I most rich. Thence comes a new intellectual exaltation, to be again rebuked by some new exhibition of character. Strange alternation of attraction and repulsion! Character repudiates intellect, yet excites it; and character passes into thought, is published so, and then is ashamed before new flashes of moral worth.

¶12   Character is nature in the highest form. It is of no use to ape it, or to contend with it. Somewhat is possible of resistance, and of persistence, and of creation, to this power, which will foil all emulation.

¶13   This masterpiece is best where no hands but nature's have been laid on it. Care is taken that the greatly-destined shall slip up into life in the shade, with no thousand-eyed Athens to watch and blazon every new thought, every blushing emotion of young genius. Two persons lately,—

very young children of the most high God,—have given me
occasion for thought. When I explored the source of their
sanctity, and charm for the imagination, it seemed as if each
answered, 'From my nonconformity: I never listened to your
people's law, or to what they call their gospel, and wasted
my time. I was content with the simple rural poverty of my
own: hence this sweetness: my work never reminds you of
that;—is pure of that.' And nature advertises me in such
persons, that, in democratic America, she will not be democ-
ratized. How cloistered and constitutionally sequestered
from the market and from scandal! It was only this morning,
that I sent away some wild flowers of these wood-gods.
They are a relief from literature,—these fresh draughts from
the sources of thought and sentiment; as we read, in an age
of polish and criticism, the first lines of written prose and
verse of a nation. How captivating is their devotion to their
favorite books, whether Æschylus, Dante, Shakspeare, or
Scott, as feeling that they have a stake in that book: who
touches that, touches them;—and especially the total soli-
tude of the critic, the Patmos of thought from which he
writes, in unconsciousness of any eyes that shall ever read
this writing. Could they dream on still, as angels, and not
wake to comparisons, and to be flattered! Yet some natures
are too good to be spoiled by praise, and wherever the vein
of thought reaches down into the profound, there is no danger from vanity. Solemn friends will warn them of the danger of the head's being turned by the flourish of trumpets,
but they can afford to smile. I remember the indignation of
an eloquent Methodist at the kind admonitions of a Doctor of
Divinity,— 'My friend, a man can neither be praised nor in-
sulted.' But forgive the counsels; they are very natural. I remember the thought which occurred to me when some
ingenious and spiritual foreigners came to America, was,

Have you been victimized in being brought hither?—or,
prior to that, answer me this, 'Are you victimizable?'

¶14   As I have said, nature keeps these sovereignties in her
own hands, and however pertly our sermons and dis-
ciplines would divide some share of credit, and teach that the
laws fashion the citizen, she goes her own gait, and puts the
wisest in the wrong. She makes very light of gospels and
prophets, as one who has a great many more to produce, and
no excess of time to spare on any one. There is a class of
men, individuals of which appear at long intervals, so emi-
nently endowed with insight and virtue, that they have been
unanimously saluted as *divine,* and who seem to be an ac-
cumulation of that power we consider. Divine persons are
character born, or, to borrow a phrase from Napoleon, they
are victory organized. They are usually received with ill-
will, because they are new, and because they set a bound to
the exaggeration that has been made of the personality of the
last divine person. Nature never rhymes her children, nor
makes two men alike. When we see a great man, we fancy a
resemblance to some historical person, and predict the se-
quel of his character and fortune, a result which he is sure to
disappoint. None will ever solve the problem of his character
according to our prejudice, but only in his own high un-
precedented way. Character wants room; must not be
crowded on by persons, nor be judged from glimpses got in
the press of affairs or on few occasions. It needs perspective,
as a great building. It may not, probably does not, form relations rapidly; and we should not require rash explanation,
either on the popular ethics, or on our own, of its action.

¶15   I look on Sculpture as history. I do not think the
Apollo and the Jove impossible in flesh and blood.
Every trait which the artist recorded in stone, he had seen in
life, and better than his copy. We have seen many counter-

feits, but we are born believers in great men. How easily we read in old books, when men were few, of the smallest action of the patriarchs. We require that a man should be so large and columnar in the landscape, that it should deserve to be recorded, that he arose, and girded up his loins, and departed to such a place. The most credible pictures are those of majestic men who prevailed at their entrance, and convinced the senses; as happened to the eastern magian who was sent to test the merits of Zertusht or Zoroaster. When the Yunani sage arrived at Balkh, the Persians tell us, Gushtasp appointed a day on which the Mobeds of every country should assemble, and a golden chair was placed for the Yunani sage. Then the beloved of Yezdam, the prophet Zertusht, advanced into the midst of the assembly. The Yunani sage, on seeing that chief, said, "This form and this gait cannot lie, and nothing but truth can proceed from them." Plato said, it was impossible not to believe in the children of the gods, "though they should speak without probable or necessary arguments." I should think myself very unhappy in my associates, if I could not credit the best things in history. "John Bradshaw," says Milton, "appears like a consul, from whom the fasces are not to depart with the year; so that not on the tribunal only, but throughout his life, you would regard him as sitting in judgment upon kings." I find it more credible, since it is anterior information, that one man should *know heaven,* as the Chinese say, than that so many men should know the world. "The virtuous prince confronts the gods, without any misgiving. He waits a hundred ages till a sage comes, and does not doubt. He who confronts the gods, without any misgiving, knows heaven; he who waits a hundred ages until a sage comes, without doubting, knows men. Hence the virtuous prince moves, and for ages shows empire the way." But there is no need to seek remote examples. He is a dull observer whose experience has not taught him the reality and force of magic, as well as of chemistry. The coldest precisian cannot go abroad without encountering inexplicable influences. One man fastens an eye on him, and the graves of the memory render up their dead; the secrets that make him wretched either to keep or to betray, must be yielded; — another, and he cannot speak, and the bones of his body seem to lose their cartilages; the entrance of a friend adds grace, boldness, and eloquence to him; and there are persons, he cannot choose but remember, who gave a transcendant expansion to his thought, and kindled another life in his bosom.

¶16   What is so excellent as strict relations of amity, when they spring from this deep root? The sufficient reply to the skeptic, who doubts the power and the furniture of man, is in that possibility of joyful intercourse with persons, which makes the faith and practice of all reasonable men. I know nothing which life has to offer so satisfying as the profound good understanding, which can subsist, after much exchange of good offices, between two virtuous men, each of whom is sure of himself, and sure of his friend. It is a happiness which postpones all other gratifications, and makes politics, and commerce, and churches, cheap. For, when men shall meet as they ought, each a benefactor, a shower of stars, clothed with thoughts, with deeds, with accomplishments, it should be the festival of nature which all things announce. Of such friendship, love in the sexes is the first symbol, as all other things are symbols of love. Those relations to the best men, which, at one time, we reckoned the romances of youth, become, in the progress of the character, the most solid enjoyment.

¶17   If it were possible to live in right relations with men! — if we could abstain from asking anything of them, from asking their praise, or help, or pity, and content us with compelling them through the virtue of the eldest laws! Could we not deal with a few persons, — with one person, — after the unwritten statutes, and make an experiment of their efficacy? Could we not pay our friend the compliment of truth, of silence, of forbearing? Need we be so eager to seek him? If we are related, we shall meet. It was a tradition of the ancient world, that no metamorphosis could hide a god from a god; and there is a Greek verse which runs,

''The Gods are to each other not unknown.''

Friends also follow the laws of divine necessity; they gravitate to each other, and cannot otherwise: —

When each the other shall avoid,
Shall each by each be most enjoyed.

Their relation is not made, but allowed. The gods must seat themselves without seneschal in our Olympus, and as they can instal themselves by seniority divine. Society is spoiled, if pains are taken, if the associates are brought a mile to meet. And if it be not society, it is a mischievous, low, degrading jangle, though made up of the best. All the greatness of each is kept back, and every foible in painful activity, as if the Olympians should meet to exchange snuffboxes.

¶18   Life goes headlong. We chase some flying scheme, or we are hunted by some fear or command behind us.

final point   But if suddenly we encounter a friend, we pause; our heat and hurry look foolish enough; now pause, now possession, is required, and the power to swell the moment from the resources of the heart. The moment is all, in all noble relations.

¶*19*
A divine person is the prophecy of the mind; a friend is the hope of the heart. Our beatitude waits for the fulfilment of these two in one. The ages are opening this moral force. All force is the shadow or symbol of that. Poetry is joyful and strong, as it draws its inspiration thence. Men write their names on the world, as they are filled with this. History has been mean; our nations have been mobs; we have never seen a man: that divine form we do not yet know, but only the dream and prophecy of such: we do not know the majestic manners which belong to him, which appease and exalt the beholder. We shall one day see that the most private is the most public energy, that quality atones for quantity, and grandeur of character acts in the dark, and succors them who never saw it. What greatness has yet appeared, is beginnings and encouragements to us in this direction. The history of those gods and saints which the world has written, and then worshipped, are documents of character. The ages have exulted in the manners of a youth who owed nothing to fortune, and who was hanged at the Tyburn of his nation, who, by the pure quality of his nature, shed an epic splendor around the facts of his death, which has transfigured every particular into an universal symbol for the eyes of mankind. This great defeat is hitherto our highest fact. But the mind requires a victory to the senses, a force of character which will convert judge, jury, soldier, and king; which will rule animal and mineral virtues, and blend with the courses of sap, of rivers, of winds, of stars, and of moral agents.

¶*20*

conclusion
If we cannot attain at a bound to these grandeurs, at least, let us do them homage. In society, high advantages are set down to the possessor, as disadvantages. It requires the more wariness in our private estimates. I do not forgive in my friends the fail-

ure to know a fine character, and to entertain it with thankful
hospitality. When, at last, that which we have always longed
for, is arrived, and shines on us with glad rays out of that far
celestial land, then to be coarse, then to be critical, and treat
such a visitant with the jabber and suspicion of the streets,
argues a vulgarity that seems to shut the doors of heaven.
This is confusion, this the right insanity, when the soul no
longer knows its own, nor where its allegiance, its religion,
are due. Is there any religion but this, to know, that, wherever in the wide desert of being, the holy sentiment we cherish has opened into a flower, it blooms for me? if none sees
it, I see it; I am aware, if I alone, of the greatness of the fact.
Whilst it blooms, I will keep sabbath or holy time, and suspend my gloom, and my folly and jokes. Nature is indulged
by the presence of this guest. There are many eyes that can
detect and honor the prudent and household virtues; there
are many that can discern Genius on his starry track, though
the mob is incapable; but when that love which is all-suffer-
ing, all-abstaining, all-aspiring, which has vowed to itself,
that it will be a wretch and also a fool in this world, sooner
than soil its white hands by any compliances, comes into
our streets and houses,—only the pure and aspiring can
know its face, and the only compliment they can pay it, is
to own it.

A Select Bibliography

STYLE MANUALS

The Chicago Manual of Style. 13th ed. Chicago: University of Chicago Press, 1982.

Jordan, Lewis, ed. *The New York Times Manual of Style and Usage: A Deskbook of Guidelines for Writers and Editors.* New York: Times Books, 1976.

Strunk, William, Jr., and E. B. White. *The Elements of Style.* 3rd ed. New York: Macmillan, 1979.

Webster's Standard American Style Manual. Springfield, Mass.: Merriam-Webster, 1985.

Words into Type. 3rd ed. Englewood Cliffs, New Jersey: Prentice Hall, 1974.

ON GRAMMAR AND USAGE

Baron, Dennis. *Grammar and Good Taste: Reforming the American Language.* New Haven: Yale University Press, 1982.

Baugh, Alfred C. *A History of the English Language.* New York: Appleton-Century-Crofts, 1957.

Bierce, Ambrose. *Write It Right,* in Bernstein, *Miss Thistlebottom's Hobgoblins.*

Bernstein, Theodore. *The Careful Writer: A Modern Guide to English Usage.* New York: Atheneum, 1986.

———. *Miss Thistlebottom's Hobgoblins.* New York: Farrar, Straus and Giroux, 1971.

Claiborne, Robert. *Our Marvelous Native Tongue.* New York: Times Books, 1983.

———. *Saying What You Mean: A Commonsense Guide to American Usage.* New York: Ballantine, 1987.

Evans, Bergen, and Cornelia Evans. *A Dictionary of Contemporary American Usage.* New York: Random House, 1957.

Follett, Wilson. *Modern American Usage.* New York: Warner, 1977.

Fowler, H. W. *A Dictionary of Modern English Usage.* 2nd ed. Oxford: Oxford University Press, 1988.

Gordon, Karen Elizabeth. *The Well-Tempered Sentence: A Punctuation*

243

Handbook for the Innocent, the Eager, and the Doomed. New Haven: Ticknor & Fields, 1983.

──────. *The Transitive Vampire: A Handbook of Grammar for the Innocent, the Eager, and the Doomed.* New York: Times Books, 1984.

Gowers, Sir Ernest. *The Complete Plain Words.* Boston: David R. Godine, 1988.

Greene, Samuel S. *The Elements of English Grammar; So Arranged as to Combine the Analytical and Synthetical Methods: With an Introduction for Beginners, and Various Exercises, Oral and Written, for the Formation, Analysis, Transformation, Clarification, and Correction of Sentences.* Philadelphia: H. Copperthwaite & Co., 1855.

Jespersen, Otto. *Growth and Structure of the English Language.* 9th ed. Garden City, N.Y.: Doubleday Anchor, n.d.

McCrum, Robert, William Cran, and Robert MacNeil. *The Story of English.* New York: Elisabeth Sifton Books/Viking, 1986.

Michaels, Leonard, and Christopher Ricks. *The State of the Language* [1980]. Berkeley: University of California Press, 1980.

Morris, William and Mary. *Harper Dictionary of Contemporary Usage.* 2nd ed. New York: Harper & Row, 1985.

Newman, Edwin. *Strictly Speaking.* Indianapolis: Bobbs-Merrill, 1974.

──────. *A Civil Tongue.* Indianapolis: Bobbs-Merrill, 1975.

──────. *I Must Say: Edwin Newman on English, the News and Other Matters.* New York: Warner, 1988.

Partridge, Eric. *Usage and Abusage: A Guide to Good English.* New York: Harper & Brothers, 1942.

Pyles, Thomas. *Words and Ways of American English.* New York: Random House, 1952.

Ricks, Christopher, and Leonard Michaels. *The State of the Language* [1990]. Berkeley: University of California Press, 1990.

Safire, William. *On Language.* New York: Times Books, 1980.

──────. *What's the Good Word?* New York: Times Books, 1982.

──────. *I Stand Corrected: More "On Language."* New York: Times Books, 1984.

──────. *Take My Word for It.* New York: Times Books, 1986.

──────. *You Could Look It Up: More "On Language" from William Safire.* New York: Times Books, 1988.

Simon, John. *Paradigms Lost: Reflections on Literacy and Its Decline.* New York: Clarkson Potter, 1980.

ON WRITING

Brockmann, R. John, and William Horton. *The Writer's Pocket Almanack.* Santa Monica, Calif.: Info Books, 1988.

Brown, Rita Mae. *Starting from Scratch: A Different Kind of Writers' Manual.* New York: Bantam, 1988.

Charlton, James, ed. *The Writer's Quotation Book: A Literary Companion.* New York: Penguin, 1986.

Charlton, James, and Lisbeth Mark, eds. *The Writer's Home Companion.* New York: Penguin, 1987.

Cook, Claire Kehrwald. *Line by Line: How to Improve Your Own Writing.* Boston: Houghton Mifflin, 1985.

Fitzgerald, F. Scott. *F. Scott Fitzgerald on Writing.* New York: Charles Scribner's Sons, 1985.

Forster, E. M. *Aspects of the Novel.* New York: Harvest/Harcourt Brace Jovanovich, 1984.

Gardner, John. *The Art of Fiction: Notes on Craft for Young Writers.* New York: Vintage, 1985.

Goldberg, Natalie. *Writing Down the Bones: Freeing the Writer Within.* Boston: Shambhala, 1986.

Hendrickson, Robert. *The Literary Life and Other Curiosities.* New York: Viking, 1981.

MacNeil, Robert. *Wordstruck.* New York: Penguin, 1990.

Plimpton, George, ed. *The Writer's Chapbook: A Compendium of Fact, Opinion, Wit, and Advice from the 20th Century's Preeminent Writers.* New York: Viking, 1989.

Read, Herbert. *English Prose Style.* New York: Pantheon, 1952.

Stegner, Wallace. *On the Teaching of Creative Writing.* Hanover, N. H.: University Press of New England, 1988.

Ueland, Brenda. *If You Want to Write.* 2nd ed. St. Paul: Graywolf Press, 1987.

Van Druten, John. *Playwright at Work.* New York: Harper & Brothers, 1953.

Welty, Eudora. *The Eye of the Story: Selected Essays and Reviews.* New York: Vintage, 1990.

————. *One Writer's Beginnings.* New York: Warner, 1985.

Winokur, Jon, ed. *Writers on Writing.* Philadelphia: Running Press, 1990.

Zinsser, William. *On Writing Well: An Informal Guide to Writing Nonfiction.* 3rd ed. New York: Harper Perennial, 1988.

————. *Writing to Learn.* New York: Harper Perennial, 1989.

SELECTED STYLISTS

Alsop, Joseph and Stewart. *The Reporter's Trade.* New York: 1973.

Barry, Dave. *Dave Barry Slept Here.* New York: Random House, 1989.

Baum, L. Frank. *The Wizard of Oz.* New York: Del Rey, 1987.

Buchanan, Edna. *The Corpse Had a Familiar Face.* New York: Random House, 1987.

————. *Never Let Them See You Cry.* New York: Random House, 1992.

Byatt, A. S. *Possession.* New York: Random House, 1990.

Chandler, Raymond. *The Simple Art of Murder.* New York: Vintage, 1988.

Cisneros, Sandra. *Woman Hollering Creek and Other Stories.* New York: Random House, 1991.

Cmiel, Kenneth. *Democratic Eloquence: The Fight over Popular Speech in Nineteenth-Century America.* New York: Morrow, 1990.

Connell, Evan S. *Mr. Bridge.* New York: Knopf, 1969.

————. *Mrs. Bridge.* New York: Viking Press, 1959.

Crane, Stephen. *The Red Badge of Courage.* New York: Vintage/Library of America, 1990.

Doctorow, E. L. *Billy Bathgate.* New York: Random House, 1989.

Eliot. T. S. *Collected Poems, 1909–1935.* New York: Harcourt, Brace, 1948.

Emerson, Ralph Waldo. *The Selected Writings of Ralph Waldo Emerson.* New York: Modern Library, 1940.

Foote, Shelby. *The Civil War: A Narrative.* New York: Random House, 1974.

Gurney, A. R. *Love Letters.* New York: Dramatists Play Service, 1989.

Gwertzman, Bernard, and Michael T. Kaufman, eds. *The Collapse of Communism.* New York: Times Books, 1990.

Hazlitt, William. *Selected Writings.* New York: Penguin, 1987.

Hemingway, Ernest. *Green Hills of Africa.* New York: Scribner Classic/Collier, 1987.

————. *The Hemingway Reader.* New York: Charles Scribner's Sons, 1953.

————. *Dateline: Toronto: The Complete "Toronto Star" Dispatches, 1920–1924.* New York: Charles Scribner's Sons, 1985.

Hughes, Langston. "Slave on the Block," in *The Norton Book of American Short Stories.* New York: W. W. Norton, 1988.

Joyce, James. *Ulysses.* New York: Modern Library, 1934.

Lessing, Doris. *The Doris Lessing Reader.* New York: Knopf, 1989.

Mailer, Norman. *The Naked and the Dead.* New York: Rinehart and Company, 1948.

Meyer, Karl E., ed. *Pundits, Poets, and Wits: An Omnibus of American Newspaper Columns.* New York: Oxford University Press, 1990.

Morrison, Toni. *Beloved: A Novel.* New York: Knopf, 1988.

Orwell, George. *A Collection of Essays.* New York: Harcourt Brace Jovanovich, 1970.

Poe, Edgar Allan. *The Complete Tales and Poems of Edgar Allan Poe.* New York: Modern Library, 1938.

Quindlen, Anna. *Living Out Loud.* New York: Random House, 1988.

Ravitch, Diane, ed. *The American Reader: Words That Moved a Nation.* New York: HarperCollins, 1990.

Ross, Lillian. *Takes: Stories from the Talk of the Town.* New York: Congdon and Reed, 1983.

Sheehan, Neil. *A Bright Shining Lie: John Paul Vann and America in Vietnam.* New York: Random House, 1988.

Sims, Norman, ed. *The Literary Journalists.* New York: Ballantine, 1984.

Smith, Logan Pearsall. *All Trivia: Trivia, More Trivia, Afterthoughts, Last Words.* New York: Ticknor & Fields, 1984.

Stone, I. F. *The I. F. Stone Weekly Reader.* New York: Vintage, 1974.

Styron, William. *Darkness Visible.* New York: Random House, 1990.

—————. *This Quiet Dust and Other Writings.* New York: Random House, 1982.

Thurber, James. *Collecting Himself: James Thurber on Writing and Writers, Humor and Himself.* New York: Harper Perennial, 1989.

Trillin, Calvin. "Covering the Cops," *The New Yorker,* February 17, 1986.

Updike, John. *Self-Consciousness.* New York: Knopf, 1989.

Vidal, Gore. *At Home: Essays 1982–1988.* New York: Random House, 1988.

White, E. B. *The Second Tree from the Corner.* New York: Harper Perennial, 1989.

—————. *Writings from "The New Yorker."* New York: HarperCollins, 1990.

Acknowledgments

Writing about anything is hard enough. Writing about writing is a daunting task. I could not have completed this book without the help of many people. Credit them with what is good in the work; credit me with all the rest: Charlotte Mayerson, an old-fashioned, hands-on editor in the grand tradition; Sharon Goldstein, who like an angel brought help and hope; and Jolanta Benal — count me now one of the many grateful writers who look forward to *her* book. Consider me fortunate to have had Kenn Russell and Amy Edelman read early drafts, Sybil Pincus proofread the galleys, Val Astor design the pages, and Sydney Cohen prepare the indexes.

I am grateful for the patient labors of the Random House Reference Department, particularly those of Jack Hornor, Lani Mysak, Judy Johnson, Chris Mohr, Joyce O'Connor, Pat Ehresmann, and Rita Rubin. Naomi Osnos and Kathy Schneider also helped this book to have a life. I thank the people who originally gave their approvals to the writing of this book: Robert Bernstein, Joe Esposito, Joni Evans, and Peter Osnos. And I extend to the Random House Copy Editing Department my admiration and appreciation for their insight into how words work: Sono Rosenberg, Nancy Inglis, Jean

McNutt, Virginia Avery, Beth Pearson, Carsten Fries, and Dennis Ambrose.

Finally, I thank three chief copy editors who taught me more than how to insert, transpose, delete, and stet: David Frost, Tory Klose, and Bert Krantz. Anyone would be lucky to have had one such mentor— lucky me, trebly blessed.

Index of Names and Titles

General Index

Permissions Acknowledgments

The authoritative dictionary of Spanish-
language usage, spelling, and pronunciation.

RANDOM HOUSE
SPANISH-ENGLISH
ENGLISH-SPANISH
DICTIONARY

DICCIONARIO
ESPAÑOL-INGLÉS
INGLÉS-ESPAÑOL

- More than 60,000 entries
- The most current spellings of the Spanish
  language academy
- Hundreds of new words, including
  código postal (zip code) and
  halterofilia (weightlifting)
- Covers Western Hemisphere usage

Consult this Spanish dictionary with confidence for the most up-to-date, reliable, and
detailed definitions available.

RANDOM HOUSE SPANISH-ENGLISH
ENGLISH-SPANISH DICTIONARY

DICCIONARIO ESPAÑOL-
INGLÉS/ INGLÉS-ESPAÑOL
by Margaret H. Raventos and David L. Gold
Published by Ballantine Books.
Available in bookstores everywhere.

The finest collection of affordable reference resources available.

RANDOM HOUSE REFERENCE

Tools to help you communicate effectively.